Bowling

Bowling

FRED BORDEN
The "Pro's Pro"
Team USA Head Coach

JOHN ACKERMAN

SERIES EDITOR
SCOTT O. ROBERTS, PH.D.
Department of Health, Physical Education, and Recreation
Texas Tech University
Lubbock, Texas

Brown & Benchmark
PUBLISHERS

Madison, WI Dubuque   Guilford, CT Chicago   Toronto London
Mexico City Caracas   Buenos Aires Madrid   Bogotá Sydney

McGraw-Hill

A Division of The McGraw-Hill Companies

Book Team

Vice President and Publisher *James M. Smith*
Senior Acquisitions Editor *Vicki Malinee*
Developmental Editor *Alyssa Naumann*
Project Manager *Dana Peick*
Production Editor *Dottie Martin*
Designer *David Zielinski*
Manufacturing Manager *Betty Mueller*
Cover Photograph *Bill Leslie*
Series Photographer *James Crnkovich*

Basal Text 10/12 Palatino
Display Type Helvetica Condensed Bold
Typesetting System Macintosh™ QuarkXPress™
Paper Stock 45# New Era Matte
Production Services Top Graphics

Brown & Benchmark
PUBLISHERS

Executive Vice President and General Manager *Bob McLaughlin*
Vice President, Business Manager *Russ Domeyer*
Vice President of Production and New Media Development *Victoria Putman*
National Sales Manager *Phil Rudder*
National Telesales Director *John Finn*

International Standard Book Number: 0-8151-0988-1

Printed in the United States of America

10 9 8 7 6 5 4 3 2 1

PREFACE

Many people do not participate in a lifetime sport, so we congratulate you on choosing bowling, whether you are just beginning to bowl or have bowled for years. You have probably chosen to participate in a lifetime sport for a variety of reasons. You may enjoy the challenge of mastering the skills and techniques of a particular sport. You may enjoy the way having an active hobby helps reduce stress in your life. You may enjoy the social aspects of participating in a sport with other people. Bowling can help you enjoy all that and more!

Bowling is a fun and challenging lifetime sport. *Bowling* is designed to provide you with a thorough understanding of the game and to help you master the techniques involved in bowling well, whether you are bowling just for fun or in competition.

▶ Audience

This text is designed for anyone who enjoys the game of bowling and plays it, as well as for students in academic courses in bowling. The book is intended to be an easy-to-read, useful tool that provides information about how to develop your game.

▶ Features

The information in this text can be used at any level of bowling proficiency. It contains basic rules and guidelines on everything from how to hold a bowling ball to how to convert spares, but it also includes a variety of drills and checklists designed to help you improve all aspects of your game. Chapter 1 introduces and defines the game, helping students to understand basics such as bowling etiquette and the layout of the lane. Chapter 2 discusses bowling equipment—everything from the way a bowling ball works to how a beginner can select the bowling equipment that's best for the individual. In this book you will learn about the rules and terminology of the game, the facilities and equipment required of the sport, and the basics of the armswing, spare conversion, and scoring. Specific drills, checklists, and tips are included throughout the book to help you improve your level of play. All directions in this book are given for both right-handed and left-handed persons.

In addition, this text offers the following special features, which enhance its use:
- Each chapter has a bulleted list of objectives and a closing summary to reinforce the major points covered.

- Key terms are highlighted in boldface type and are also defined. This feature enables you to build a working vocabulary of concepts and principles necessary for beginning, developing, and maintaining your game.
- Performance Tip boxes outline techniques, applications, and strategies for quick reference.
- Assessments appear at the end of applicable chapters to assist you in evaluating your skill and game performance.
- The Appendix provides a list of rules to help bowlers make sure that their play conforms to the rules of the game.
- Professional photographs illustrate proper techniques for effective bowling and complement the text discussion.

▶ Ancillaries

To facilitate the use of this text in the classroom, a printed Test Bank of approximately 100 questions is available to instructors. These questions, ranging from true/false to brief-answer formats, allow for quick assessment of the basic rules and principles of bowling.

▶ Acknowledgments

We would like to thank the following reviewers, who provided us with expert commentary during the development of this text:

John E. Dollar, Ph.D.
Texas A&M University, College Station

Tim Ruden, M.S.
Iowa State University, Ames

Dean A. Whited, Ph.D.
North Dakota State University, Fargo

We would also like to extend a special thanks to the entire bowling community for the opportunity to teach and coach the basics and the finer aspects of our great sport.

—Fred Borden
John Ackerman

CONTENTS

Bowling

CHAPTER 1

WHAT'S BOWLING ALL ABOUT?

OBJECTIVES

After reading this chapter, you should be able to do the following:

- Define and explain the object of the game of bowling.
- List and explain in general terms the components of a typical bowling center.
- List and explain the primary rules of bowling etiquette.
- Describe a lane in general terms.
- Identify and explain the purpose of the components of a lane.
- List and explain major bowling safety precautions.

KEY TERMS

While reading this chapter, you will become familiar with the following terms:

- ▶ Approach
- ▶ Back End
- ▶ Ball Return

- ▶ Bowling Area
- ▶ Bowling Center
- ▶ Channels

Continued

KEY TERMS

- ▶ Concourse
- ▶ Control Desk
- ▶ Foul Line
- ▶ Frames
- ▶ Head Pin
- ▶ Heads
- ▶ House Ball
- ▶ Lane
- ▶ Lay-Down Point

- ▶ Open Frame
- ▶ Perfect Game
- ▶ Pin Triangle
- ▶ Pines
- ▶ Spare
- ▶ Splice
- ▶ Strike
- ▶ Target Arrows

BOWLING DEFINED

In fundamental terms bowling is defined as a game in which bowlers use a bowling ball to knock down pins arranged at the end of a lane.

OBJECT OF THE GAME

From the definition you can see that the object of the game involves knocking down pins, but it is a bit more complicated than that. Let's take a closer look.

In bowling, a *game* consists of 10 **frames.** A frame in bowling is similar to an inning in baseball. During a frame you get two chances to knock down all the pins. One of three things happens when you bowl a frame:

- If you knock down all the pins on your first shot, you have made a **strike** and you don't take a second shot.
- If you leave pins standing on the first shot but knock them down on the second shot, you have made a **spare.**
- If there are pins still standing after you take your second shot, you have made an **open frame.**

Scoring strikes and spares gives you extra rewards or bonuses that are applied to your score.

- An open frame is worth the number of pins you knocked down in the frame.
- A spare is worth 10 points plus your next shot.
- A strike is worth 10 points plus your next two shots.
- Your total score is the number of pins you knocked down plus the bonus points you earned for strikes and spares you made during the game. If you score strikes in all frames, your score is 300 points, or a **perfect game.**

BOWLING CENTERS

A **bowling center** is the place where bowling takes place. A modern bowling center offers much more than just bowling; it is a place where family and friends gather to enjoy a game of bowling along with refreshments and meals. Some bowling centers offer other activities in which family members who are not bowling can participate. Examples of these activities are billiards, a video game room, a pro shop, a lounge or sports bar (often with live entertainment or karaoke), and meeting rooms.

Some bowling centers offer outdoor activities such as golf or miniature golf, volleyball, go-cart race tracks, and various other activities you can enjoy.

Although they are not identical in size, construction, or services offered, most bowling centers have at least four parts: a **control desk,** lanes, a **bowling area,** and a **concourse.** The heartbeat of most bowling centers is the control desk, where you check in to receive a lane assignment, receive your score sheet, rent shoes, and get answers to any questions you may have about bowling or the bowling center. Bowling takes place on lanes (you will learn more about lanes later in this chapter). The bowling area is a place behind the lanes where bowlers wait to bowl. A typical bowling area has a number of seats located at its rear perimeter and a desk on which to keep score. The concourse is the area behind the lanes and bowling area where spectators sit and bowlers leave food and drinks between frames. Most bowling centers do not allow food and drinks in the bowling areas.

▶ **Frames**

Measurements of the game's progress, similar to innings in baseball. Every game of bowling consists of 10 frames.

▶ **Strike**

A term used to describe your score when you knock down all the pins with one roll of your bowling ball.

▶ **Spare**

A term used to describe your score when you knock down all the pins in two consecutive rolls of your bowling ball.

▶ **Open Frame**

A term used to describe your score when you fail to knock down all pins in two consecutive rolls of your bowling ball.

▶ **Perfect Game**

The maximum points you can attain in a game of bowling: 300. A perfect game oc-curs when all 12 balls that you roll in a game score a strike.

▶ **Bowling Center**

The facility in which you enjoy a game of bowling.

▶ **Control Desk**

The area in a bowling center where you make the arrangements and receive the equipment you need to begin a game.

▶ **Bowling Area**

The area behind the lane where the bowlers wait to bowl.

▶ **Concourse**

The area behind the lanes where spectators sit.

Caring for a bowling center is everyone's responsibility, not just the proprietor's. Remember that the condition of a bowling center reflects on the public perception of bowlers and the sport of bowling. Respect the established rules of the bowling center. Although the rules may not be the same in all bowling centers, complying with them is simply a matter of good manners. Remember: "When in Rome . . . ."

BOWLING ETIQUETTE

When you go to a bowling center, you expect to have a good time. That means enjoying the companionship of your friends, relaxing in the center's pleasant atmosphere, and getting some good exercise while you develop your bowling skills.

Nothing can spoil a great attitude (not to mention a potentially great game) faster than having an annoying person in the lane next to you. The main ingredient to bowling etiquette is a mutual respect between bowlers and others who are in the bowling center. The basic, commonsense rules of bowling etiquette are discussed in the following paragraphs.

WHO BOWLS FIRST?

The general rule is the first person up bowls first. If there is any question as to who was first up, the bowler on your right should bowl first.

WHEN IT'S YOUR TURN—BE READY!

Once you are lined up in your stance and ready to bowl, don't wait; just go. Many bowlers get in the stance and fixate themselves on the pins until they feel they have it right. Remember, you can't knock down pins by staring at them, you have to deliver the ball!

During fast-paced competition, people tend to quickly get annoyed with a person who hesitates in the stance. Moreover, as you will learn later, hesitation does not promote a proper mental game. Chances are that if you hesitate in the stance, you tend to overthink and end up getting psyched out.

The time for thinking about your shot is before you line up in the stance. Once you step on the lane's approach, don't hesitate; take your shot.

If the lanes are crowded and others are waiting to bowl, don't wait at the foul line to see the results of your shot.

BE CONSIDERATE

Be especially considerate toward your teammates and bowlers in the lanes on either side of your lane. Part of the camaraderie is giving and taking. A little ribbing from time to time is acceptable, but don't overdo it.

AVOID PROFANITY

Bowling is a wholesome family sport, so don't use profanity in the bowling center. Do have a good time, but try not to be overly loud or rowdy.

ESTABLISH A POSITIVE ATTITUDE

One of the keys to bowling excellence is a positive attitude. A negative attitude does more than just aggravate your teammates; it adversely affects your performance.

LANE

All bowling takes place on a **lane.** An important thing to remember is that *all lanes are created equal*, thanks to the American Bowling Congress (ABC), the Women's International Bowling Congress (WIBC), and the Bowling Proprietors Association of America. Every bowling lane in the world is the same width (42 inches from channel to channel) and the same length (64 feet from the foul line to the back row of pins). The boards that make up the lane are spaced the same distance apart (about 1 inch), and the locator dots and target arrows (discussed shortly) are always in the same place, five boards apart. Figure 1-1 shows the layout and dimensions of a typical lane.

▶ **Lane**
The place where you actually bowl.

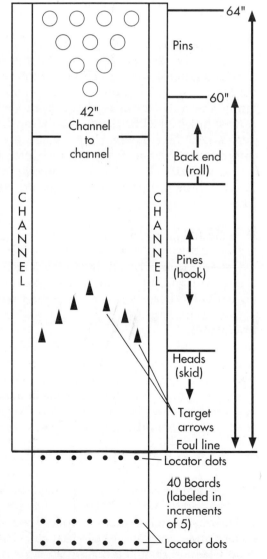

FIGURE 1-1 Typical lane layout.

COMPONENTS OF A LANE

A lane can be divided into six components: the approach, the channels, the heads, the pines, the back end, and the pin triangle.

▶ Approach

The **approach** is the area that begins at the front of the lane and ends at the **foul line.** It is here that you assume your stance and make your shots. The foul line is the line of demarcation between the heads and is used as the limit of your forward advance when you make a shot. Any pins you knock down are not counted if your feet go beyond the foul line.

▶ Channels

Two **channels,** one on each side of the lane, run from the foul line to the rear of the pin triangle. Channels receive a ball that rolls off the lane and direct it past the pins to the end of the lane. Channels are sometimes referred to by their slang term: *gutters.* Adjacent to the channels is the lane's **ball return.** The ball return serves two purposes: to hold bowling balls in a circular or straight ball rack and to return the ball from the pin area to the ball rack after a bowler has taken his or her shot. The majority of ball returns are simply underground tubes that use gravity to transport the ball to the ball rack. Ball returns are situated between two lanes so that two lanes are served.

▶ Heads

The area from the foul line to the target arrows is called the **heads.** The heads usually are made up of hard maple wood to withstand the constant impact of bowling balls. The heads are sometimes referred to as the *skid area.*

▶ Pines

The area beginning at the end of the heads and running down the lane to the back end is called the **pines** because it is made of soft pine wood. The pines take far less punishment from bowling balls than do the heads because the ball normally never impacts the pines; it hooks on it. The area where the hard maple wood of the heads meets the soft wood of the pines is called the **splice.**

▶ Back End

The rearmost part of a lane is called the **back end** and consists of two parts: the roll area and the pin deck. The hook area comprises the first 15 feet of the back end and is constructed of soft pine wood. The soft pine allows the ball to "grab" the lane surface and curve into the pin triangle. The pin deck occupies a 4-foot area immediately behind the roll area. The pin deck is made of hard maple wood to support the pins and withstand the impact of flying pins when struck by a bowling ball.

LANE SURFACES

Bowling centers regularly apply a dress coating of a special oil to the lane, with more oil usually applied to the heads than to the pines. The back ends are cleaned regularly. After several hours of play, bowling balls tend to carry oil with them into the back ends, making them oily as well. When this happens, the oil is usually stripped off and a fresh coating is applied.

It is interesting to note that lanes are finished to high tolerances to ensure that they are flat and smooth. The lanes are sanded to within 20 thousandths of an inch flatness. Urethane coatings are usually applied twice each year to maintain the lanes in top condition.

The three alternate names for the heads, pines, and back end (*skid, hook,* and *roll*) are used because, ideally, your bowling ball should skid through the heavily oiled heads; start to hook (move toward the head pin) when it reaches the softer, lightly oiled pines; and roll when it hits the dry back end. A combination of forces acts as a ball skids, starts to hook, and rolls that causes the ball to curve into the pins.

One problem is that the oil conditioner regularly applied to the lanes doesn't stay where applied. It evaporates. Often, because of drafts, overhead lighting, and other conditions, certain areas evaporate faster than others. Also, as the bowling balls roll down the lanes they carry oil with them, depositing it on the presumably dry back end. This is the reason why although every lane is physically identical, a bowling ball won't roll the same way on every lane. This is known as the *condition*

▶ **Approach**

The area that begins at the front of the lane and ends at the foul line. It is here that you assume your stance and make your shots.

▶ **Foul Line**

The line of demarcation between the approach and the heads. The foul line is used as the limit of your forward advance when making a shot. Any pins knocked down are not counted if your feet go beyond the foul line.

▶ **Channels**

U-shaped tracks on either side of a lane designed to receive and "channel" a ball that rolls off a lane past the pins to the end of the lane. Sometimes referred to as *gutters.*

▶ **Ball Return**

A part of a lane designed to return a bowler's ball from the pin area back to the ball rack at the front of the lane.

▶ **Heads**

The area of a lane from the foul line to the target arrows. The heads usually are made up of hard maple wood to withstand the constant impact of bowling balls. Sometimes referred to as *skid area.*

▶ **Pines**

The area of a lane between the heads and the back end or the midsection of the lane.

▶ **Splice**

The area of a lane where the hard maple wood of the heads meets the soft wood of the pines.

▶ **Back End**

The rearmost part of a lane, consisting of two parts: the hook area and the pin deck.

of a lane, which you must learn to adjust to. After you roll your ball down a lane a few times, you will be able to determine the lane's condition and make adjustments accordingly.

PIN TRIANGLE

The area in which the pins are placed on the lane is called the **pin triangle** and holds the 10 pins arranged in four rows. Figure 1-2 shows how the pins are arranged inside the pin triangle. Pins are referred to by number (1 through 10). The #1 pin is called the **head pin.** Pins are always numbered from left to right, so the #2 and #3 pins make up the second row of the triangle. Pins #4 through #6 make up the third row, and pins #7 through #10 are in the fourth row.

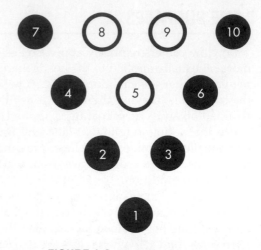

FIGURE 1-2 Pin triangle.

Like lanes, pins are uniform in size, shape, and weight. Each pin is 15 inches tall, has a circumference of 15 inches, is approximately 4¹¹⁄₁₆ inches in diameter, and must weigh between 3 pounds, 6 ounces, and 3 pounds, 10 ounces. Weight variance in each set of pins may not exceed 4 ounces. Each pin has two hollow areas, giving it a topple angle of approximately 9 degrees.

TARGET ARROWS

Embedded in the boards on the lane are seven **target arrows,** which are located 15 to 17 feet from the foul line. These target arrows aid you in lining up for a shot.

- For right-handed bowlers, the arrows are numbered from *right to left.*
- For left-handed bowlers, the arrows are numbered from *left to right.*

In relation to the lane, the target arrows are spaced one every five boards from the middle (#4 target arrow). Each target arrow is directly aligned with a respective outside pin in the pin triangle, as shown in Figure 1-3.

This relationship between the target arrows and the outside pins is hard to detect with your eyes. The reflective surface of the lane, as well as the distance to the pins, often creates the illusion that they are not aligned. Be assured, though, that they are.

LOCATOR DOTS

The four sets of locator dots include three sets before the foul line and one set after the foul line (see Figure 1-3).

For now, we will concentrate on the three sets of locator dots before the foul line or on the approach. As you read the next few paragraphs, refer to Figure 1-3 to better understand the importance of locator dots.

The first two sets of dots are spaced 15 and 12 feet before the foul line. They are designed to help you line up properly in your stance. As with the target arrows, each locator dot is spaced five boards from the next. In some bowling centers there will be seven locator dots: three to either side of the large center dot. Other bowl-

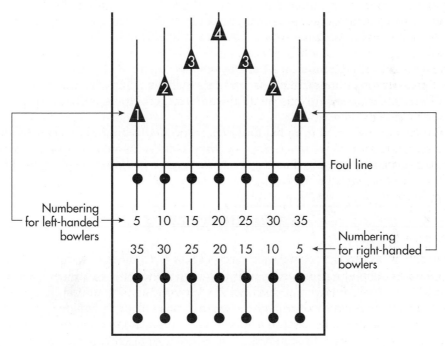

FIGURE 1-3 Target arrows and locator dots.

▶ **Pin Triangle**
The area of the lane on which the 10 pins are arranged in a triangular, four-row pattern.

▶ **Head Pin**
The #1 pin in the pin triangle.

▶ **Target Arrows**
Arrow shapes embedded into the boards on a lane, 15 to 17 feet from the foul line. Target arrows aid you in lining up for a shot.

ing centers will have only five dots: two on either side of the large center dot. The farthest dot on each side has been eliminated on lanes with five dots.

Theoretically, the set of dots 15 feet before the foul line is where a five-step approach bowler should assume the stance. The set of dots 12 feet away from the foul line is where a four-step approach bowler assumes the stance. (These two approach techniques will be covered later in this text.) Since everyone's walking gait is different, this is not a rule you should follow but a place to start.

The third set of locator dots is located 2 to 3 inches before the foul line. This set of dots is helpful in determining the amount of drift during your approach, your angle to the lane, and the point on the lane where your ball lands when you make a shot (the **lay-down point**).

Vertically, these dots are arranged in a straight line with each other. In other words the middle dot 15 feet from the foul line lines up with the middle dot that is 2 to 3 inches from the foul line. Each dot in a set is aligned with the dot in front of it.

Not only do these dots line up with each other; they also line up with both the target arrows and the outside pins of the pin triangle. The middle dot is in line with the middle target arrow, which also is in line with the head pin. The next dot to the right is in line with the third target arrow, which is in line with the #3 pin. The next dot to the right is in line with the second target arrow, which is in line with the #6 pin. The same relationship exists with the dots, target arrows, and outside pins on the left side of the lane.

Out on the lane, 7 feet from the foul line, respectively, are 10 other locator dots. Don't worry about these dots right now; they will be covered later on. Once you start bowling, you will use them to fine-tune your target line to achieve better accuracy and bowling proficiency.

BOWLING SAFETY

According to the U.S. Consumer Product Safety Commission, approximately 17,000 cases of bowling-related injuries that require hospital treatment occur each year. This is a relatively small number since more than 70 million people bowl every year. Even though your chances of injury are small compared to other sports, accidents still happen. Bowling is a sport, and, with all sports, injury may result if basic safety practices are not followed. The following paragraphs cover most of the safety precautions you should be aware of before you begin to bowl.

AVOID MOISTURE ON YOUR SHOES

Moisture is probably your number one enemy when you bowl. The smooth rubber and leather on bowling shoes get sticky even if they are slightly wet. Since your approach ends with your feet sliding, wet soles can be treacherous. The accompanying box tells how to avoid this problem.

Performance Tip

Avoiding Moisture on Your Shoes

- On rainy or snowy days, don't leave the bowling area more than necessary.
- Be sure to keep food and beverages out of the bowling area.
- Watch where you walk when you leave the bowling area. Remember that the moisture you deposit on the approach is a hazard for you and your teammates as well.
- Sometimes new bowling shoes stick to the approach even when they are dry. To solve this problem, use a knife and some sandpaper to round and smooth the leading edge of the heel of your sliding shoe. In extreme cases, placing a piece of nonstick (Teflon) tape to the leading edge of the sliding shoe's heel will correct the problem.
- Do not enter the bowling area wearing your street shoes. Doing so could introduce moisture and dirt to the bowling area and approach. Change into your bowling shoes first.
- Consider purchasing shoe protectors to put over your bowling shoe's slide when you have to leave the bowling area to visit the snack shop or rest room. Shoe protectors are available at the bowling center's pro shop or retail area.

BOWLING BALL SAFETY

It may sound ridiculous to say, "Don't drop the ball on your foot," but many great bowlers have accidentally done just that. A bowling ball is a smooth, heavy object that can easily slip from your grasp if you are not careful. The box on p. 13 lists some rules to follow when handling a bowling ball.

▶ **Lay-Down Point**
The place on a lane where your ball lands when you make a shot.

Performance Tip

Don't Use Baby Powder on Your Bowling Shoes!

Don't make the mistake made by many bowlers of using baby powder on the soles. Not only is it illegal—it's dangerous!

COMMON SENSE IS THE KEY

Obviously, the best way to prevent injuries is to be aware of what is going on around you and use common sense.

- After bowling a shot, make sure to walk on your side of the approach. Some people tend to watch their shots while walking backward from the foul line. Drifting to the right or left as you walk backward can put you in another person's way.
- When you are not bowling, stay clear of the ball return area until it is your turn to bowl. Some bowlers swing their bowling ball or their arm as they go through their preshot routine. You could get bumped accidentally.

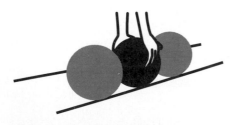

FIGURE 1-4 Picking up a bowling ball.

FIGURE 1-5 Cradling the ball.

Performance Tip

How to Handle a Bowling Ball Safely

- Always dry your hands with a towel or use the air blowers on the ball return.

- When you pick up a ball from the return, grasp it by the sides as shown in Figure 1-4. This prevents pinched fingers in case another ball comes out of the return unexpectedly.

- Don't put your fingers in the ball holes when you pick it up and carry it. Conserve the strength in your right hand and fingers for actual bowling. Instead, after you pick up the ball, cradle it in your left arm as shown in Figure 1-5. (If you bowl left-handed, cradle the ball in your right arm.)

- When using a **house ball** (which, by the way, is provided free of charge) at the bowling center, make sure the ball you select has a thumb hole slightly larger than the finger holes. This ensures a clean release of your thumb so that your fingers will impart a rotation on the ball.

- Use a lighter rental ball rather than the heaviest one available. You will understand why when we discuss ball weights later in this book.

- Be careful when you lift your bowling bag. Many bowlers carry two or more bowling balls in their bags, in addition to shoes, wrist aids, and other equipment. The weight of the bag plus the weight of the equipment can easily exceed 50 pounds. When you lift your bag, keep your back straight, bend at the knees and waist, and use the big muscles of your legs. Also, keep the weight of the bag close to your body.

▶ **House Ball**

A bowling ball supplied to you free of charge by the bowling center. House balls are stored in readily accessible ball racks near the control desk. House balls vary in weight, hole size, and grip size to accommodate virtually any bowler's preferences.

SUMMARY

- The game of bowling consists of 10 frames, similar to innings in baseball. During a frame, you get two chances to knock down all the pins.
- You bowl in a bowling center, a facility dedicated to the game. Typical parts of a bowling center are the control desk, concourse, and bowling area.
- Bowling, like any other sport, has established rules of play and etiquette.
- You bowl on a specific area of the bowling center, a lane. No matter where you bowl, all lanes have the same dimensions and parts.
- The major parts of a lane are the approach, heads, pines, back end, and pin triangle.
- Lanes contain built-in aids (target arrows and locator dots) that help you line up and aim your ball.
- Bowling, like any other sport, can be hazardous unless you follow commonsense safety precautions.

CHAPTER 2

THE RIGHT EQUIPMENT:
VITAL TO THE GAME

OBJECTIVES

After reading this chapter, you should be able to do the following:

- Identify the equipment you need to enjoy the sport of bowling.
- Explain the fundamental rules for choosing the proper equipment.

KEY TERMS

While reading this chapter, you will become familiar with the following terms:

- ▶ Ball Balance
- ▶ Bridge
- ▶ Core
- ▶ Finger Weight
- ▶ Hook
- ▶ Pitch
- ▶ Porosity

- ▶ Shell
- ▶ Skid
- ▶ Span
- ▶ Thumb Weight
- ▶ Weight Block
- ▶ Weight Hole

BOWLING BALL BASICS

A bowling ball is composed of three parts: the **shell, core,** and **weight block.** Figure 2-1 shows these parts.

The shell is the outside covering of the ball. The shell is hard and durable so that it can withstand landing on the lanes and impacting the pins. The core is the center of the bowling ball. On top of the core is a piece of dense, heavy material: the weight block. The weight block adds weight to the ball at the top to compensate for the loss of weight at the top caused by the drilling of the thumb and finger holes.

Bowling balls usually are drilled with three holes for the thumb, middle finger, and ring finger. (Actually, you are allowed to have one more hole drilled in a ball other than holes used to grip the ball. This is called a **weight hole** and is used by advanced bowlers to adjust their ball for specific applications.) Figure 2-2 shows the placement of the holes.

The distance between the two finger holes is called the **bridge,** and the distance between the thumb hole and the finger holes is called the **span. Pitch** refers to how the holes are drilled in relation to the center of the ball. When you purchase your personal bowling ball, the ball driller will make sure that the hole's pitch is perfect for your hand.

All bowling balls are 27 inches in circumference (approximately 9 inches in diameter). The weight of a bowling ball varies from 6 to 16 pounds. According to the American Bowling Congress (ABC), the Women's International Bowling Conference (WIBC), and Young American Bowling Alliance (YABA) regulations, a bowling ball cannot weigh more than 16 pounds.

Various markings on the outside of a bowling ball usually include the manufacturer's logo, the brand name of the ball, a serial number, and a small dot showing where the top of the weight block is located. Some bowlers also have their names engraved on their bowling ball. On a house ball (a ball provided by the bowling center), the weight of the ball is usually marked above the finger holes.

The box on p. 17 provides a few guidelines for helping you select a house bowling ball.

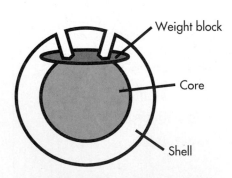

FIGURE 2-1 Parts of a bowling ball.

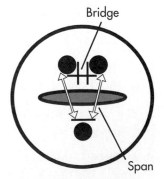

FIGURE 2-2 Placement of holes in a bowling ball.

Performance Tip

Things to Remember When Selecting a Ball

As a beginning bowler, you will probably use a house ball. Remember that every bowling ball has its own serial number. When you find a house ball that works well for you, remember the serial number so you can find it the next time you bowl.

BALL GRIP

Holes are drilled in bowling balls by drillers at a bowling pro shop. Drillers are skilled specialists, many of whom have bowled professionally. A good ball driller will work with you to customize a ball that will fit you perfectly and add to your bowling performance.

▶ **Shell**
The outside covering of a bowling ball. The shell is hard and durable so that it can withstand landing on the lanes and impacting the pins.

▶ **Core**
The material making up the center of a bowling ball.

▶ **Weight Block**
A piece of dense, heavy material that adds weight to a bowling ball at the top to compensate for the loss of weight at the top caused by drilling the thumb and finger holes.

▶ **Weight Hole**
An additional hole drilled in a bowling ball used by advanced bowlers to adjust their ball for specific applications.

▶ **Bridge**
A term used to describe the distance between a bowling ball's two finger holes.

▶ **Span**
A term used to describe the distance between a bowling ball's thumb hole and finger holes.

▶ **Pitch**
A term used to describe how the thumb and finger holes are drilled in relation to the center of the ball.

FITTING

Your bowling ball, whether a personal or house ball, should fit properly. You want the finger and thumb holes to be snug enough so you won't drop the ball, yet loose enough to afford a smooth release. The thumb hole should be slightly looser than the finger holes since the thumb comes out of the hole first during the release.

The accompanying box contains information you can use to achieve a better fitting bowling ball.

HAND FIT

The ball must fit your hand properly for optimal performance. The three items of importance in determining a proper fit are hole size, span, and pitch.

▶ Hole Size

The thumb hole should be slightly looser than the finger holes. This allows your thumb to release first and your fingers last. When your thumb releases first, your fingers tend to "lift" the ball out onto the lane. The distance between the two finger holes (bridge) should be about ¼ to ⅜ inch.

▶ Span

The distance between the thumb hole and finger holes determines the ball's span. How you determine a proper fit relative to span depends on the size of your hand and which type of grip you use. (We'll cover types of grip shortly.)

Comfort is the key. Note the web of skin between your thumb and index finger. When you are using a properly fitted ball, the web should be neither taut nor slack.

Performance Tip

How to Make Your Bowling Ball Fit Better

The weather has an effect on bowling ball fit. Usually your hands are somewhat larger when it's warm and smaller when it's cold. If the holes are too big, place a strip of black electrician's tape (cloth type, not plastic) in the back of the holes to make them smaller. If you prefer, you can buy bowler's tape that is cut to shape and size in the bowling center's pro shop.

▶ **Pitch**

Pitch is the offset among the thumb hole, finger holes, and the ball's centerline. Pitch is determined when the ball is drilled: inward for a smaller, weaker hand and outward for a stronger hand.

TYPES OF GRIPS

The three basic types of grips are conventional, semi-fingertip, and fingertip. With a conventional grip the holes are drilled deeper so that your fingers and thumb enter up to the second knuckle of your hand. With a semi-fingertip grip the holes are drilled so that your fingers fit up to midway between the second and first knuckles. With a fingertip grip your fingers fit up to the first knuckle. The fingertip grip is the most shallow grip. Figure 2-3 shows these three types of grips.

Beginning and infrequent bowlers (those who bowl less than once per week) usually use the conventional grip. As you become more experienced and truly want to excel in the sport, you should adopt a fingertip grip. The fingertip grip is used by more than 99% of professional bowlers. The fingertip grip encourages a quicker, smoother thumb and finger release than the conventional grip. You can apply better turn and lift to your bowling ball using a fingertip grip.

Using the semi-fingertip grip is not recommended because your hand doesn't contact the bowling ball properly, creating a gap where your fingers bend into the holes.

The box on p. 20 contains information on checking the span fit for a conventional grip.

BALL COVER

When we talk about ball cover, we mean cover texture or finish. Some balls have a dull finish; others are shiny. A bowling ball's finish refers to its **porosity.** Balls with a high porosity are dull and scratchy. Balls with a low porosity are bright and shiny. To achieve porosity, bowling ball covers are made of polyester, hard rubber, polyurethane, or polyurethane with a reactive resin ad-

▶ **Porosity**
A term used to describe a bowling ball's outer cover finish.

Conventional

Semi-fingertip

Fingertip

FIGURE 2-3 Types of grips.

Performance Tip

How to Check Span Fit for a Conventional Grip

Place your thumb all the way into the ball's thumb hole, and then place your fingers over the finger holes. Your knuckles should extend ¼ to ⅜ inch past the front edge of the finger holes (the edge closest to the thumb hole).

ditive. Polyurethane balls have higher porosity characteristics than polyester, hard rubber, or reactive resin polyurethane. Simply speaking, a ball's porosity tends to define its **hook** characteristics. Hook is the action imparted by a bowler to a bowling ball that causes its path down a lane to curve toward the head pin. For right-handed bowlers the ball curves to the left. For left-handed bowlers the ball curves to the right. The amount of hook a ball imparts also depends on the lane's condition. A drier lane produces more hook, and an oily lane produces less hook.

On a lane, balls with different porosities act differently. A high-porosity ball will bite into the surface of the lane and provide better traction and hook characteristics. A low-porosity ball will **skid** more and hook less. Skid is the sliding action of a bowling ball on a lane before it grips the lane's surface and begins to hook. Skid characteristics vary on each lane and from day to day because of lane usage, weather, and the smoothness of the lane before oil is applied.

You can use a ball's porosity coupled with lane conditions to improve your performance. (We'll cover this in more detail later.) If lane conditions are dry, you may be getting more hook than you want. Switching to a shinier (low-porosity) ball will help reduce your hook. If lane conditions are oily, you may not be getting enough lane traction to cause your ball to hook. Using a dull (high-porosity) ball will increase traction and the ball's potential to hook. The box on p. 21 will help you determine the hook and traction characteristics of a bowling ball.

BALL WEIGHT

Two factors must be considered when we talk about ball weight. The first is the weight itself. You need to use a ball that is the proper weight for you. The second is the relationship between the weight block and the thumb and finger holes, a term referred to as **ball balance.**

Balls range in weight from 6 to 16 pounds. Which is correct for you?

A general rule of thumb is to *use the heaviest ball you can control without sacrificing accuracy or ball speed.* Generally speaking, a lighter ball traveling faster is sometimes

Performance Tip

Determining a Ball's Hook and Traction Characteristics

- High-porosity balls provide better lane traction and more hook. Use a high-porosity ball on an oily lane.

- Low-porosity balls provide less lane traction and less hook. Use a low-porosity ball on a dry lane.

- You can change a ball's traction and hook characteristics by having the local pro shop sand or polish your ball.

better than a heavier ball traveling slower. We can prove this by using a rule of physics to calculate a ball's momentum.

Let's assume that your ball weighs 10 pounds and you can release it with enough force to make it travel down the lane at 15 miles per hour. Calculate the ball's momentum using this formula:

$$\text{Ball mass} \times \text{Ball velocity} = \text{Ball momentum}$$

where ball mass is the weight of the ball in pounds and ball velocity is the speed of the ball in miles per hour.

$$10 \times 15 = 150$$

Now let's change the ball's weight to 12 pounds and its speed to 10 miles per hour.

$$12 \times 10 = 120$$

So you can see that a faster, lighter ball carries more momentum than a heavier, slower one. What does this mean to you? It means that the faster, lighter ball will

▶ **Hook**
The action imparted by a bowler to a bowling ball that causes its path down a lane to curve toward the head pin.

▶ **Skid**
The sliding action of a bowling ball on a lane before it grips the lane's surface and begins to hook.

▶ **Ball Balance**
The relationship between a bowling ball's weight block and its thumb and finger holes.

strike the pins at a greater momentum than the slower, heavier ball. The additional momentum results in more pin action.

To be effective a ball must have some friction with the lane surface. How you achieve this friction largely depends on making sure you select a ball that is the proper weight for you. If you use a ball that is too light it will travel too fast and slide or skid on the top of the lane. When the ball hits the pins, the lack of friction causes it to deflect off the pins, resulting in reduced pin action and fewer pins knocked down. Conversely, if you use a ball that is too heavy for you, its speed is too slow to generate pin action so it deflects off the pins.

Once more, comfort is the key. Try different balls until you see which is best for you. Ask your instructor to help you evaluate which ball to use.

▶ Weight Block and Weighting

As you begin to bowl, you will hear terms such as right side weight, positive weight, or finger weight. This might lead you to believe that a ball driller adds weight to a ball to achieve these weights. This is not true; drillers do not add weight to a ball. Instead, they take out weight when they drill the holes. From 1 to 3 ounces of material is removed when the holes are drilled.

According to ABC/WIBC regulations, the top of a bowling ball can weigh up to 3 ounces more than the bottom after the holes are drilled. In addition, weight can vary up to 1 ounce in any direction from the center.

If the holes are drilled to the left of the weight block (to the left of the manufacturer's label) there will be more weight on the ball's right-hand side. This ball has *right side weight*. The opposite is true if the holes are drilled to the right of the weight block; the ball has *left side weight*. However, if the holes are drilled directly over the top of the weight block, the ball has *no side weight*.

Balls with right side weight are often referred to as having *positive weight*, whereas balls with left side weight have *negative weight*. This is reversed if you are left-handed. Figure 2-4 shows how side weight is achieved when a bowling ball is drilled.

Experienced bowlers put right or left side weight on a ball to affect its reaction on a lane. This is why all professional bowlers use more than one ball.

Beginning bowlers should use a ball having no side weight until they gain experience in the game.

▶ Thumb and Finger Weight

Thumb and finger weight describes the relationship between the holes and the weight block. If the center of the weight block is closer to the finger holes, a ball has **finger weight.** If the center of the weight block is closer to the thumb holes, a ball has **thumb weight.** Figure 2-5 shows how thumb or finger weight is achieved when a bowling ball is drilled. Determining which is best for you is a trial and error process. You should work with the ball driller to see which is best for you. In theory, finger weight makes a ball skid longer, whereas thumb weight makes a ball roll earlier.

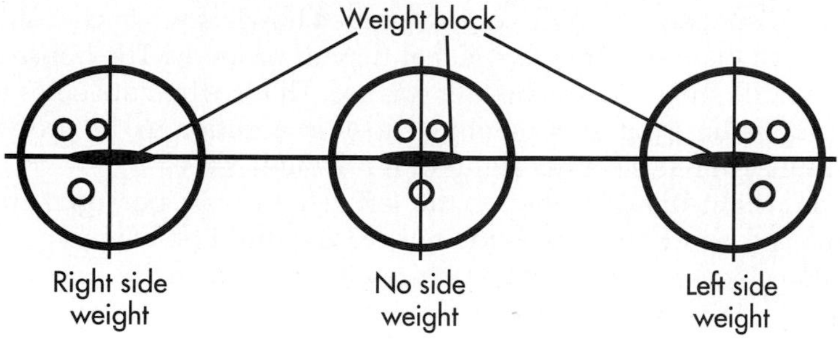

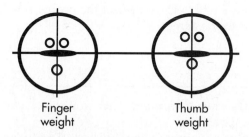

FIGURE 2-4 Side weight.

FIGURE 2-5 Finger and thumb weight.

▶ **Finger Weight**

A term used to describe the relationship between a bowling ball's holes and the weight block. If the center of the weight block is closer to the finger holes, a ball has finger weight.

▶ **Thumb Weight**

A term used to describe the relationship between a bowling ball's holes and the weight block. If the center of the weight block is closer to the thumb holes, a ball has thumb weight.

BOWLING SHOES

Bowling shoes are an important contributor to your performance on the lanes. You have two choices for bowling shoes: those provided at the bowling center (house shoes) or those that you purchase. There are some interesting differences between the house shoes and those that you purchase.

The right and left soles of the house shoes are leather. Leather soles enable you to slide easier when you get to the foul line. When you purchase a pair of bowling shoes only one of the soles will be made of leather. The reason for this depends on whether you are a right- or left-handed bowler.

There is no distinction for right- or left-handed bowlers when choosing a pair of house shoes. All that really matters is that they fit properly. The house shoe is essentially a generic shoe that any bowler can use. That's why both soles are leather.

When you purchase a pair of bowling shoes, in addition to the proper size and width, you must purchase either right- or left-handed shoes.

If you are a right-handed bowler, the left sole of your personal shoe will be leather. This is the foot that you slide toward the foul line when you release the ball. The other sole is made of rubber to provide traction on the approach. The opposite is true for left-handed bowling shoes.

SELECTING THE PROPER EQUIPMENT

The following pointers will help you select the proper bowling ball and shoes, both of which are vital to the game.

BOWLING BALL

Here are some things to keep in mind when you select a bowling ball, either a house ball or your personal ball:

- Choose a ball that is the proper weight for you. Use the heaviest ball you can control without sacrificing accuracy or ball speed.
- If you are a beginner, choose a ball that has a conventional grip and no side weight.
- Select a ball that has the porosity characteristics that make it perform on the lanes you bowl on.
- Use a dull (high-porosity) ball on oily lanes.
- Use a shiny (low-porosity) ball on dry lanes.
- When you decide to purchase a ball, work closely with the ball driller to make sure you get the ball that will perform well for you.

▶ What Type of Bowling Ball Should You Own?

There are 27 possible bowling ball weights and cover combinations to match the 27 lane conditions you might encounter (we will discuss these in detail later in this text). This doesn't mean that you should buy 27 bowling balls to match them. A beginner does well with one bowling ball. A fairly serious bowler can get along well with two bowling balls. An advanced or professional bowler may own as many as 6 to 24 bowling balls.

Beginning Bowlers. Let's say you started bowling a few months ago. Now, you're in a league or two, you've developed your style to a fair degree, and you're eager to have a bowling ball of your own so you can improve performance and consistency. The best bowling ball for you would be a medium cover with no side weights, finger weights, or thumb weights. This means the ball would be drilled so that the weight block would be equidistant from all the holes. A medium cover, polyester ball should prove satisfactory under most lane conditions and would be much less expensive than a polyurethane ball.

You would adjust to lane conditions by moving right or left in your stance, closing or opening your shoulders, and using the advance wrist techniques you will learn about later on.

Serious Bowlers.   A serious bowler is a person who normally bowls two or three times per week and has done so for at least 1 year. Serious bowlers would want to own two bowling balls: one for oily lane conditions and one for dry lane conditions.

For oily lane conditions a serious bowler would have a polyurethane or reactive resin polyurethane ball (high-porosity surface). This ball would be finger weighted and have either positive right side weight or no side weight (left side weight for left-handed bowlers).

For dry lane conditions a serious bowler would have a polyester ball (low-porosity surface). This ball would be finger weighted and have either positive side weight or no side weight (left side weight for left-handed bowlers).

If you are bowling in lane conditions between oily and dry, you could use whichever of the two balls you felt most comfortable with and whichever best complemented your game and the angle you like to play.

Advanced and Professional Bowlers.   Advanced or professional bowlers would want to have approximately six bowling balls to match the lane conditions on tour. With these six balls, advanced or professional bowlers would be able to adjust to any lane condition they would encounter. Don't worry about this yet; we want you to be aware of the value of equipment.

BOWLING SHOES

The accompanying box gives pointers that will help you select the proper bowling shoe.

Performance Tip

Selecting Bowling Shoes That Are Right for You

- Select a pair of shoes that properly fit in both size and width. A good rule to follow is to select a pair of shoes that are the same as your street shoe size and width.

- When you purchase a pair of bowling shoes, choose the proper size and width and be sure to specify either right or left depending on whether you are a right- or left-handed bowler.

SUMMARY

- To be a successful bowler, you must select the equipment that is right for you and fits properly.
- By understanding how your equipment helps you become a successful bowler and the fundamental rules for selecting equipment, your bowling skills will improve with experience and practice.

CHAPTER 3

FOCUS ON **STANCE:** PREPARING TO PERFORM

OBJECTIVES

After reading this chapter, you should be able to do the following:

- Describe and explain the importance of a proper stance.
- Explain where to line up.
- Explain how to line up.
- Describe how various parts of your body should be positioned in the stance.
- Demonstrate a proper stance and line-up.

KEY TERMS

While reading this chapter, you will become familiar with the following terms:

- ▶ Initial Position
- ▶ Money Shot
- ▶ Strike Pocket
- ▶ Suitcase Position
- ▶ Target Line
- ▶ Tempo

STANCE: AN OVERVIEW

▶ A vpttrvy dysmvr of vtivos;o

No, this isn't a foreign language. It's what can happen when a typist or word processor places his or her hands on the wrong starting positions before typing. Instead of constantly watching the keyboard, experienced typists and word processors place their hands in the correct keyboard starting position before they begin. Through years of practice, they know exactly where all the other keys are in relation to that initial keyboard position.

If the hands are first placed properly on the keyboard, the "foreign language" above makes sense.

▶ Correct Stance Is Crucial!

If you are new to bowling, the points this lesson covers may seem like a lot to remember at first. After the first few times at the bowling center, you will note that a correct stance simply feels right. Soon you will naturally assume a proper stance without any conscious thought.

Practice makes perfect. At the end of this chapter is an at-home balance drill for the stance that you can use to develop your stance. Two stance checklists, one for right-handed bowlers and one for left-handed bowlers, can also be found at the end of this chapter. We recommend that you use them because they will help you develop and refine your stance.

WHERE TO LINE UP

The two things to consider when determining where to line up are your distance from the foul line and your position to the right or left of the large center locator dot.

Two marks on the approach will help you determine where to line up: the foul line and the locator dots. Figure 3-1 shows you where these marks are on the lane.

DISTANCE FROM FOUL LINE

As a general rule, a person 5 feet tall would want to line up on the second set of locator dots in front of the foul line. This will vary, though, according to a person's height. A taller person will want to line up farther away than a shorter person because a taller person usually has a longer stride.

The box on p. 30 shows a simple method you can use to precisely determine how far away from the foul line to line up. Figure 3-2 shows how to perform this method.

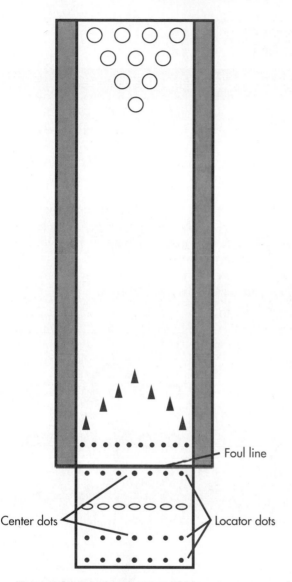

FIGURE 3-1 Foul line and locator dots.

POSITION TO RIGHT OR LEFT

If you are right-handed, line up with your *left* foot 1 inch or so to the *right* of the center locator dot. If you are left-handed, line up with your *right* foot 1 inch or so to the *left* of the center locator dot.

The box on p. 31 shows how you can locate your initial stance position.

This is the **initial position** where you line up when making strikes. If you have lined up properly, your ball will describe a path to an area within the pin triangle known as the **strike pocket.** Later in this text, you will learn how to shift the initial position back and forth to make spares. You will also learn how to adjust this position to compensate for lane conditions. Figure 3-3 shows how your feet should be positioned relative to the locator dot when you are in the initial position. For right-handed bowlers, line up the right side of your left shoe relative to the locator dot. The reverse is true for left-handed bowlers.

▶ **Initial Position**

A place on the approach where you line up when making strikes. If you have lined up properly, your ball will describe a path to the strike pocket.

▶ **Strike Pocket**

An area in the pin triangle where, if your ball were to enter, would give you the best possible chance of making a strike. Normally, the strike pocket is the area between the head pin and #3 pin for right-handed bowlers and between the head pin and #2 pin for left-handed bowlers.

Performance Tip

Determining Where to Line Up

1. Line up facing *away* from the pins with your heels approximately 2 inches from the foul line.
2. If you are right-handed, start with your right foot and take 4½ brisk steps. If you are left-handed, start with your left foot and take the same amount of steps. Don't turn around yet.

   The four steps take into account the four steps you will use for your approach. The extra half step accounts for the slide you make at the end of your approach. The steps also give you some leeway so you won't go over the foul line when you finish your approach.
3. Now turn around and face the pins by pivoting with the foot in front of you (in other words, do an about-face). This is the position on the approach where you should line up.

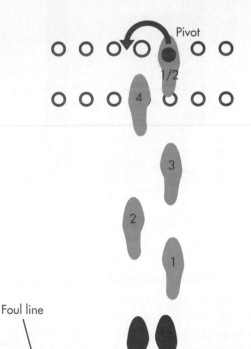

FIGURE 3-2 Take 4½ steps and pivot.

Performance Tip

Locating Your Initial Stance Position

When you practice, move right and left in the stance about 1 inch at a time (or one board) until you find the spot that is perfect for you. You will know when you have found the perfect spot because more pins will fall.

Center dot   Center dot

FIGURE 3-3 Position of feet relative to the locator dot.

Left-handed bowler   Right-handed bowler

BODY POSITION: WAIST DOWN

▶ **Feet**

If you bowl right-handed, position your *right* foot about 5 inches in back of your *left* foot. This will help give you better balance in the stance. This position helps you start your approach more naturally since you will be moving your right foot first. If you bowl left-handed, position your *left* foot about 5 inches in back of your *right* foot. Figure 3-4 shows this position in relation to the center locator dot.

Left-handed bowler   Right-handed bowler

▶ **Knees**

When you line up in the stance, *flex* your knees slightly. After all,

FIGURE 3-4 Stance position to the left or right.

you are an athlete preparing to execute a series of fluid movements. Avoid locking your knee joints. Instead, bend and relax them.

How far should you bend your knees? To answer this question, consider this: How far would you bend your knees if you were catching a bag of potatoes dropped from a truck? Try to picture that scenario in your mind because it will give you a good mental picture of how much you should bend your knees.

A good rule of thumb is to tilt your knees forward about 10 to 15 degrees so they extend out toward your toes about 4 to 6 inches. Figure 3-5 shows the amount of knee bend you should have in the stance.

Remember to keep your knees flexed throughout your approach without straightening up.

FIGURE 3-5 Bend your knees.

BODY POSITION: WAIST UP

▶ Spine

When it comes time to bowl, you are going to move forward. To help prepare yourself, the weight of your body should be positioned forward. Tilt your spine forward about 15 degrees and make sure you maintain this position throughout your approach and delivery. Figure 3-6 illustrates this position.

▶ Shoulders

When you bowl, the weight of your bowling ball is on one side of your body. It is only natural that the weight of one shoulder will be a little lower than the other.

If you bowl right-handed, let your *right* shoulder drop a few inches lower than your *left*. If you bowl left-handed, let your *left* shoulder drop a few inches lower than your *right*. Figure 3-7 shows how your shoulder should be positioned in the stance.

FIGURE 3-6 Tilt your spine forward.

FIGURE 3-7 Let your shoulder drop.

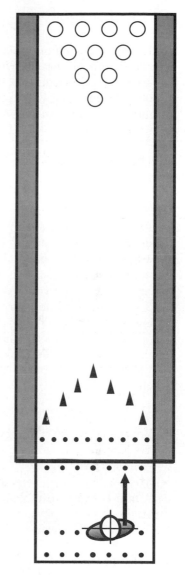

It has been said that we could all bowl better if our eyes were on top of our shoulders. Then we would be able to see the precise path our ball would follow. Although this is obviously impossible, you can still develop a good mental picture of your ball's path.

Here's how. The path your ball takes down the lane is the **target line.** Picture the target line as the *line in your mind.* Then try to keep this picture in your mind when you bowl. As you take your stance, imagine a 3-foot arrow resting on your shoulder. Align this arrow with the line in your mind. With this mental picture, you have determined the path your ball will take when you release it. Figure 3-8 shows how the line should look if you imagined it correctly.

FIGURE 3-8 Picture the line in your mind.

▶ **Target Line**
An imaginary mental picture of a line that follows the path of your bowling ball.

▶ Arms

Make sure the elbow of your arm holding the ball is resting against your side. Use your other hand to help cradle and support the ball while you are in the stance. Figure 3-9 shows how your arms should be positioned while in the stance.

FIGURE 3-9 Arm position in the stance.

WHERE TO HOLD THE BALL

If you have watched other bowlers, you have probably noticed that some hold the ball at chest level, and others hold it at hip level or below. Both these positions (and any in between) are correct. Where you hold the ball depends on your bowling **tempo,** or how fast you get to the foul line in the approach. The faster you are, the lower you hold the ball. This helps you synchronize your armswing to your footsteps during the approach.

A slow bowler should hold the ball at chest level. A medium speed bowler should hold the ball at waist level. A fast bowler should hold the ball below the waist. Figure 3-10 depicts ball position relative to bowling tempo.

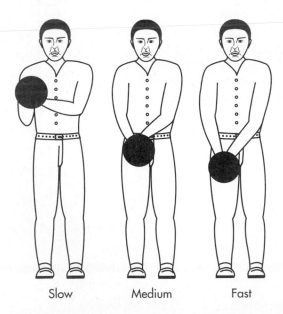

Slow   Medium   Fast

FIGURE 3-10 Ball position relative to bowling tempo.

HOW TO HOLD THE BALL

In the stance the weight of your ball should rest against the pincher muscles of your bowling hand and your other hand should help support the weight of the ball, as shown in Figure 3-11. When you cradle the ball in this way, the little fingers of each hand should touch.

You may have a question about what fingers go in what holes and in what order you put them there. First, place your middle finger and ring finger in the two finger holes. Then place your thumb in the larger thumb hole last, because you want the thumb to come out of the ball first. Figure 3-12 shows where to place your fingers.

Later you will learn different ways to position the ball in your hand, but for now you will learn about the easiest position for beginners: the **suitcase position.**

FIGURE 3-11 Holding the ball.

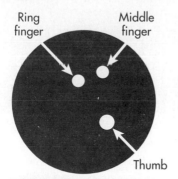

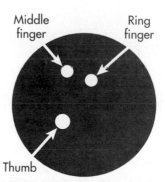

Left-handed bowler   Right-handed bowler

FIGURE 3-12 Finger/thumb placement *(top view).*

▶ **Tempo**
The speed at which you get to the foul line on your approach.

▶ **Suitcase Position**
Term used to describe a method of holding the ball on your approach. It is described this way because you hold the ball much the same way you would hold and carry a suitcase.

Imagine that you are holding the handle of a suitcase. This is how you should position your hand when holding the bowling ball. The suitcase delivery is also referred to as the **money shot** because your thumb faces your pants pocket during the armswing. In the suitcase position your little finger should be close to your ring finger to promote a slight rotation of your hand at the point of release. Figure 3-13 shows how your hands should be positioned for a suitcase delivery.

Another way to visualize this is to imagine the face of a clock around your bowling ball. If you bowl right-handed, your thumb should be in the 10-o'clock position. If you bowl left-handed, your thumb should be in the 2-o'clock position. Figure 3-14 illustrates this for right- and left-handed bowlers.

FIGURE 3-13 Suitcase position.

FIGURE 3-14 Suitcase thumb positions *(back view).*

Left-handed bowler   Right-handed bowler

▶ **Wrist**

Keep your wrist straight throughout your stance, approach, and release. You may notice that some advanced bowlers cup their wrist to give the ball more spin. Others break (we don't mean this literally!) to make the ball go straighter. Figure 3-15 shows the cupped, straight, and broken wrist positions. Cupped and broken wrist positions are advanced techniques to be tried only after you have mastered the straight wrist position.

BOWLING BALANCE

If you follow all the guidelines discussed in this chapter, you should feel relaxed, balanced, and natural in the stance.

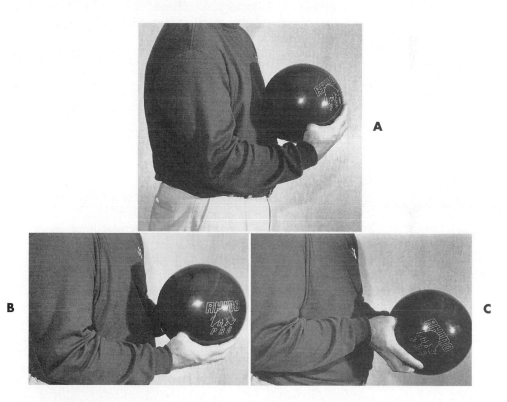

FIGURE 3-15 **A,** Cupped, **B,** straight, and **C,** broken wrist positions.

▶ **Money Shot**
Term used to describe the results of a suitcase position shot. It is described this way because your thumb faces your pants pocket (where your money is) during the approach and release.

Performance Tip

Perceiving the Rocking Motion

The rocking motion should not be noticeable to the eye; just enough so that you can feel it.

When in the stance, your weight should be balanced on the balls of your feet. Just before you begin your approach, rock back on your heels *slightly*, then forward as you begin to take your first step. Figure 3-16 shows how you should assume this position.

The accompanying box clarifies how the rocking motion should feel.

SUMMARY

- The stance has basic rules that show you where to line up, how to line up, and the body position you should assume.
- The suitcase position is the most common way to hold the ball in the stance.
- A proper stance is important because it prepares you for the approach.

FIGURE 3-16 Assume a relaxed, balanced natural position.

Assessment 3-1

At-Home Balance Drill for Stance

Name _____   Section _____   Date _____

This section contains assessment activities in the form of checklists and drills you can use to develop and perfect your stance. Do the at-home balance drill for the stance first; then go to the stance checklists.

Here's a drill you can do at home that will help you put into practice what you learned in this chapter. We recommend you try it. To perform this drill you will need a full-length mirror and a bowling ball.

1. Stand in front of a full-length mirror so you can see a reflection of yourself from a side view.
2. Without holding your bowling ball, line up in the stance and take a few deep breaths.
3. Close your eyes and mentally check your stance posture starting at your feet and working your way up to your head. Feel your weight balanced and centered slightly on your feet.
4. Now open your eyes and review your image in the mirror. How does it compare with your mental image?
5. If you note any differences, correct them and repeat the drill, starting with step 1.
6. Repeat the drill four times, correcting any discrepancies you note between your mental image and your actual stance.
7. Now perform the drill five more times while holding your bowling ball.

The stance checklists in Assessment 3-2 can help you develop a better stance. Two stance checklists are provided: one for right-handed bowlers and one for left-handed bowlers.

Assessment 3-2

Name   Section   Date

A stance checklist is similar to the preflight checklist that an airplane pilot must go through before taking off. The time to check the gas tanks of a plane is not at 5000 feet. Neither can your stance position be evaluated halfway down the lane.

Although there is a lot to remember to achieve a proper stance, a stance checklist makes it simple. Take this checklist with you when you bowl. If you are a beginning bowler, review the stance checklist before and after you bowl a frame.

If you use this checklist faithfully, your stance posture and positioning will become a subconscious act. Automatically, your mind will start at your feet and work its way up, making sure that every part of your body is poised and ready for action.

Two stance checklists are provided: one for right-handed bowlers and one for left-handed bowlers.

RIGHT-HANDED BOWLER'S STANCE CHECKLIST

1. Feet
   _____ Correct alignment with the locator dots
   _____ Facing target
   Four-step approach
   _____ Feet together
   _____ Left foot slightly in front of right foot with right foot inside the arch of left foot
   Five-step approach
   _____ Inside edge of left toe lined up with the back inside portion of the right heel
2. Knees
   _____ Bent at 20-degree angle (no bowing in or out)
3. Spine
   _____ Bent forward at waist 15 degrees
4. Shoulders
   _____ Three-foot arrow off right shoulder pointed directly at the target line
   _____ Shoulders perpendicular to the target line
   _____ Straight with the rest of your body (no twisting of your body)
   _____ Right shoulder 2 inches lower than left shoulder
5. Right elbow
   _____ Against side just beneath where rib cage cuts in
6. Left arm
   _____ Left elbow bent in front of the body about 3 to 4 inches in front of right elbow

     _____ Left hand cradling left portion of ball
     _____ Little fingers touching (beginners)

7. Right wrist
     _____ Cupped, straight, or broken (beginners use straight wrist)

8. Right hand
     _____ Under ball
     _____ Proper grip

9. Ball placement
     _____ Horizontal placement: middle of ball 2 inches to the inside of right hip
     _____ Vertical placement: height above or below waist (beginners use waist height)
     _____ Placement of ball in hands: determined by type of ball thrown (hook or straight)

10. Head
     _____ Straight relative to body
     _____ Pointed toward target
     _____ Tilted slightly forward and down

11. Eyes
     _____ Focused solely on target

12. Overall balance
     _____ Center of body weight on balls of feet
     _____ (optional) Use rock-back technique just before starting approach

LEFT-HANDED BOWLER'S STANCE CHECKLIST

Name _____ Section _____ Date _____

1. Feet
   _____ Correct alignment with the locator dots
   _____ Facing target
   Four-step approach
   _____ Feet together
   _____ Right foot slightly in front of left foot with left foot inside the arch of right foot
   Five-step approach
   _____ Right toe lined up with back inside portion of left heel
2. Knees
   _____ Bent at 20-degree angle (no bowing in or out)
3. Spine
   _____ Bent forward at waist 15 degrees
4. Shoulders
   _____ Three-foot arrow off left shoulder pointed directly at the target line
   _____ Shoulders perpendicular to the target line
   _____ Straight with the rest of your body (no twisting of your body)
   _____ Left shoulder 2 inches lower than right shoulder
5. Left elbow
   _____ Against side just beneath where rib cage cuts in
6. Right arm
   _____ Right elbow bent in front of the body about 3 to 4 inches in front of left elbow
   _____ Right hand cradling right portion of ball
   _____ Little fingers touching (beginners)
7. Left wrist
   _____ Cupped, straight, or broken (beginners use straight wrist)
8. Left hand
   _____ Under ball
   _____ Proper grip
9. Ball placement
   _____ Horizontal placement: middle of ball 2 inches to the inside of right hip
   _____ Vertical placement: height above or below waist (beginners use waist height)
   _____ Placement of ball in hands: determined by type of ball thrown (hook or straight)
10. Head
    _____ Straight relative to body
    _____ Pointed toward target
    _____ Tilted slightly forward and down
11. Eyes
    _____ Focused solely on target

12. Overall balance
    _____ Center of body weight on balls of feet
    _____ (optional) Use rock-back technique just before starting approach

Started Earth Slides

CHAPTER 4

FOCUS ON **APPROACH:**
FOUR STEPS TO SUCCESS

OBJECTIVES

After reading this chapter, you should be able to do the following:

- Describe and explain the four-step approach.
- Discuss where to aim during the approach.
- Explain and discuss in fundamental terms the elements of the release and fol-
  low-through.
- Discuss some of the common approach problems and their cures.
- Describe and explain the five-step approach.

KEY TERMS

*While reading this chapter, you will become familiar with the follow-
ing terms:*

- ▶ **Backswing**
- ▶ **Double Dribble**
- ▶ **Push-Away**
- ▶ **Rocking Chair Syndrome**
- ▶ **Stance Position**

FOUR STEPS TO FOUL LINE: FOUR-STEP APPROACH

Before reading this section, study the contents of the accompanying box, which discusses the basic technique for the approach.

Of the different types of approaches, the most common is the four-step approach. The four-step approach is recommended for beginners because it provides a foundation on which to build accuracy.

We present the four-step approach by numbering each step and then relate the numbers to the position of the bowling ball at the end of each step. Five separate positions are covered. The first is the **stance position.** For this discussion the stance position is the 0:0 position. Figure 4-1 shows the 0:0 position. Note that the position of the bowler's right foot is numbered 0 and shown in relation to the ball position, which is also numbered 0.

You begin the steps of your approach from the 0:0 position.

FIGURE 4-1 Stance (0:0) position.

STEP 1: POSITION 1:1

During the first step your right foot steps forward as your right arm simultaneously pushes the ball out and down toward your right foot. At the end of the first step, the ball should be poised above your right foot. Your left hand should continue to help support the ball throughout this step. Figure 4-2 illustrates step 1.

Performance Tip

Remember Basic Technique for the Approach

Although this chapter breaks down the approach into four or five basic steps, you should perform them in one fluid motion. A successful approach occurs when your body and mind work as one in a free-flowing series of coordinated movements.

FIGURE 4-2 Step 1: position 1:1.

Keep these two points in mind during step 1:
1. Make sure that your leg and arm move at the same time. If the ball and your foot don't end up in the 1:1 position simultaneously, your timing will be off throughout the approach.
2. Move the ball straight out toward the lane so that it ends up over your right foot. Don't let it veer to the right or left. This movement is often referred to as the **push-away,** because you *push* the ball *out* toward the lane and *down* toward the floor. *If you bowl left-handed,* move your *left* foot forward as your *left* hand pushes the ball out toward the lane and over your foot.

▶ **Stance Position**

The first position in the sequence in which the approach is presented in this text. Also the 0:0 position because the position of the bowler's right foot is numbered 0 and shown in relation to the ball position, which is also numbered 0.

▶ **Push-Away**

A movement performed during the approach, because you *push* the ball *out* toward the lane and *down* toward the floor.

STEP 2: POSITION 2:2

During the second step your left foot moves forward as the ball arcs down. Your left hand should leave the ball at the beginning of the step. At the end of this step, the ball should end up beside your right calf. Figure 4-3 illustrates step 2.

If you bowl left-handed, move your *right* foot forward as the ball arcs down. Your *right* hand should leave the ball at the beginning of the step.

FIGURE 4-3 Step 2: position 2:2.

STEP 3: POSITION 3:3

During the third step, your right foot moves forward as the ball arcs back to the highest point of your armswing, which should be about shoulder height. Figure 4-4 illustrates step 3.

If you bowl left-handed, move your *left* foot forward as the ball arcs back to the height of your armswing.

FIGURE 4-4 Step 3: position 3:3.

FIGURE 4-5 Step 4: position 4:4.

STEP 4: POSITION 4:4

During the fourth step, your left foot moves forward into the slide as the ball arcs down. At the end of the fourth step, the ball should be in the lowest part of your armswing. Your right arm should be pointed directly at the floor and ready to release the ball. Figure 4-5 illustrates step 4.

If you bowl left-handed, move your *right* foot forward and position it for the slide while the ball arcs down.

As the ball starts down during this step, your right foot should slide sideways in back of your left leg. Simultaneously, you should "sit down" or lower your hips slightly and position your weight so you end up in a comfortable sitting position with your lower body and spine tilted forward about 15 degrees. Figure 4-6 illustrates this position.

If you bowl left-handed, your *left* foot should slide sideways in back of your *right* leg.

Make sure you do not slide over the foul line during the fourth step. If you slide over the foul line during competition (and release the ball) you receive no points for the shot.

FIGURE 4-6 Finish position and slide.

OVERVIEW OF RELEASE
AND FOLLOW-THROUGH

After you complete the fourth step, and during the slide, you should continue through the release and follow-through without hesitation. An overview of the release and follow-through is presented next so you will be familiar with basic release and follow-through techniques. A more detailed discussion on the release and follow-through is presented in Chapter 6.

There are three parts to the release:

1. Just after the fourth step, your thumb should release from the ball. If you are still holding the ball correctly in the suitcase position (remember Chapter 3?), your thumb should drop out of the ball naturally.
2. Your fingers, which are still in the holes, should continue to lift out and up. With your hand in the suitcase position, this should impart a natural sideways spin to the ball, causing it to hook slightly into the pins.
3. Your fingers should release smoothly from the ball as your hand and swing continue arcing out and up in the follow-through.

Figure 4-7 illustrates the parts of the release.

Your follow-through should result in a finish position with your hand still aligned with the target line as shown in Figure 4-8.

FIGURE 4-7 Three parts of the release.

FIGURE 4-8 Following through to the finish position.

WHERE TO AIM

Although this text will cover taking aim in later chapters, you would probably like to practice and want to know where to aim for a strike. Figure 4-9 shows a bowling lane with the target arrows discussed in Chapter 1. Remember that the target arrows are numbered from right to left if you bowl right-handed, or from left to right if you bowl left-handed.

For now, aim for the second target arrow. If you use the suitcase release, the ball should hook into the strike pocket (for right-handed bowlers, this is the right side of the #1 pin, or head pin). This is the best place to hit the pins so they will create a perfect domino effect to make a strike.

If your shot consistently misses the strike pocket to the right or left, move your initial position in the direction of the miss. For example, if your ball misses the strike pocket a little to the right, move your initial position in the stance a little to the right. If it misses to the left, move your initial position to the left.

TROUBLESHOOTING ACCURACY PROBLEMS

Although other keys to accuracy will be covered later, one of the biggest factors that affects accuracy is the position of your shoulders.

As you learned in Chapter 3, imagine a 3-foot arrow balanced on the shoulder of your bowling arm and aligned with the target line your ball will follow down the lane (the line in your mind). Make sure your shoulders remain aligned with the target line in the stance, throughout your approach, and during the release and follow-through.

SHOULDER POSITION RELATIVE TO LANE

We often refer to your shoulders and how they should be positioned relative to the lane. Your shoulders can be opened, closed, or square in relation to the lane. If your shoulders are opened, they are turned away or to the right of the center pin. If your shoulders are closed, they are turned in or to the left of the center pin.

You want your shoulders nearly perfectly square to the lane when you attempt to make a strike. Adopt this position in the stance and maintain it throughout the approach and delivery. Figure 4-10 shows shoulder position for right- and left-handed bowlers.

The box on p. 54 contains some things you need to remember about your position relative to the lane.

Often the problem of opening or closing your shoulders is a matter of improper timing. Problems with timing usually begin with the first step of your approach.

If your armswing is slower than your feet, your arm will end up in the **backswing** when you take the fourth step. This unsynchronized movement contorts your body and opens your shoulders when you release. Your ball will miss to the right if you are right-handed and to the left if you are left-handed.

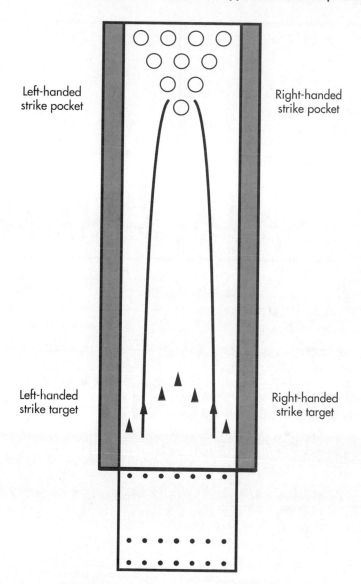

FIGURE 4-9 A lane and target arrows.

▶ **Backswing**
That portion of the armswing when your arm moves backward relative to your body.

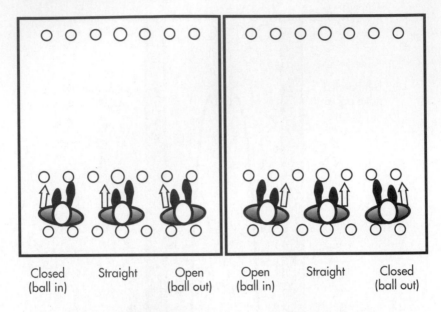

Closed (ball in)   Straight   Open (ball out)   Open (ball in)   Straight   Closed (ball out)

Left-handed bowler   Right-handed bowler

FIGURE 4-10 Closed, straight (square), and open shoulder positions.

Performance Tip

Remember Your Position Relative to the Lane

- Open shoulders = ball out. For right-handed bowlers the ball will miss the strike pocket to the right. For left-handed bowlers the ball will miss to the *left*.
- Closed shoulders = ball in. For right-handed bowlers the ball will miss the strike pocket to the left. For left-handed bowlers, the ball will miss to the *right*.

The opposite happens if your armswing is faster than your feet. This twists your body, closes your shoulders, and causes you to release the ball before you finish the fourth step and slide. The result is a miss to the left if you are a right-handed bowler or a miss to the right if you are a left-handed bowler.

An anonymous bowler once said, "A great start equals a great finish." Most timing problems can be cured during the first step. Make sure to move your hand and foot as one during the first step. This may seem difficult at first, but with practice you will soon be doing it naturally.

If you still have problems with timing your armswing to your feet movements, try raising the ball or lowering the ball in the stance. We covered this in Chapter 3, but the accompanying box should refresh your memory.

AVOID ROCKING CHAIR SYNDROME

Some bowlers have a problem rocking their shoulders forward and backward during their approach. This results in erratic ball behavior and inaccurate bowling known as the **rocking chair syndrome.**

If your shoulders rock forward during the fourth step and release, the ball will impact the lane behind the foul line, bounce back up, and hit the lane again. This phenomenon is often called **double dribble.**

If your shoulders rock back during the fourth step and release, the ball will loft out and impact the lane well beyond the foul line. A little loft on the ball is good, but only a little. A good loft distance is approximately 18 to 24 inches out onto the lane.

The cure to these shoulder problems is to perform the approach with your spine tilted at the same 15-degree angle you assumed in the stance. You can imagine this by picturing yourself trying to balance a cup of coffee on your shoulders. Try not to spill a drop during your approach and release.

Performance Tip

Compensating for Timing Problems

- If your armswing is faster than your feet movements, raise the ball to chest level.

- If your armswing is slower than your feet movements, lower the ball to waist level.

▶ **Rocking Chair Syndrome**
A problem some bowlers experience by rocking their shoulders forward and backward during their approach that results in erratic ball behavior and inaccurate bowling.

▶ **Double Dribble**
Action that occurs if your shoulders rock forward during the fourth step and release because the ball impacts the lane behind the foul line, bounces back up, and hits the lane again.

AVOID DRIFTING

Be careful not to drift to the right or left during your approach. Drifting is another major contributing factor to inaccuracy. Check where your feet are located after a shot. You should end up with your feet within one or two boards of where you lined up in the stance. Whether to drift or walk straight to the foul line has been a matter of discussion for several years. To ensure the accuracy of your shot, we recommend walking straight to the foul line on every shot.

The locator dots where you place your feet in the stance are lined up with the locator dots before the foul line. This means that if you line up in the stance with your left foot beside the center dot, you should end up with your left foot beside the center dot when you reach the foul line.

The number one reason for drifting, however, is your armswing. If your arm wraps in behind your body, you will drift left. If your arm swings out away from your body, you will drift right. Remember that accuracy is not possible unless your armswing is straight. Chapter 5 discusses more about armswing and how to control it.

FIVE-STEP APPROACH

You may have heard about the five-step approach. Essentially, this approach is the same as the four-step approach except that you take an initial, "getting started," baby step at the beginning. The ball does not move from its stance position when you take this step.

If you bowl right-handed, start this small step with your *left* foot. If you bowl left-handed, start it with your *right* foot.

After this initial step, the five-step approach is exactly the same as the four-step approach. You may want to review the four-step approach discussed earlier in this chapter.

The accompanying box contains a bit of wisdom concerning the five-step approach.

Performance Tip

Using the Five-Step Approach

If you use the five-step approach, make sure to give yourself a bit more room from the foul line to allow for the extra baby step.

CHOOSING FOUR- OR FIVE-STEP APPROACH

You might be asking the question, "What approach should I use?" Here are some reasons to help you decide.
- A smaller person may want to use five steps to achieve a longer and faster approach.
- A larger (and stronger) person would choose a five-step approach to achieve a shorter and slower approach.

You can see by these examples that a four-step approach can help you gain momentum and a four-step approach can help you slow down.

The bottom line is simply this: Which approach is easiest for you? Try both at home first and then at your local bowling center. Don't be afraid to experiment. You will soon discover the approach that is best for you.

SUMMARY

- The four-step approach is the most common and easiest to perfect. The five-step approach is used by more experienced bowlers.
- Locator dots are the key to aiming your shot on the approach.
- A good approach must be accompanied by an equally good release and follow-through.
- Because of its complexity, you can experience problems with your approach. These problems can be eliminated by constant practice and evaluation.
- Choose the approach that is easiest for you, but only after practicing them extensively.

• • •

The following assessments will help you to check your start and approach. The two practice drills for your start include one for right-handers and one for left-handers. There are two practice drills for your timing, posture, and approach: a weight transfer drill and an approach drill. Checklists for the approach are also given in this section, one for right-handed bowlers and one for left-handed bowlers.

Assessment 4-1

Practice Drills for the Start

Name   Section   Date

Try this practice drill three nights each week for 3 weeks. At the end of 3 weeks, you will note an improved start when you are actually bowling.

As you perform this exercise, make sure that your forearm is aligned and square with your body. Focus on synchronizing the motions of your hands and feet.

RIGHT-HANDED START DRILL

1. Imagine that you are holding your bowling ball, and align yourself in the stance. Close your eyes, and take a few deep breaths.
2. Breathe in while shifting back slightly and transferring your weight to your right heel.
3. For a *four-step approach*, exhale slowly and transfer your weight to the ball of your left foot. As your weight becomes centered on the ball of your left foot, take your first step with your right foot as you move your ball into the push-away.

   For a *five-step approach*, exhale slowly while you slide your left foot forward into the baby step. *Do not move your ball as you take this sliding baby step.* Then take your second step with your right foot while moving the bowling ball into the push-away.
4. Repeat this drill five times without holding anything in your hand. Then repeat it five more times while holding your bowling ball. If you don't have a bowling ball, use an object that simulates a bowling ball, such as an iron.

LEFT-HANDED START DRILL

Name   Section   Date

1. Imagine that you are holding your bowling ball, and align yourself in the stance. Close your eyes, and take a few deep breaths.
2. Breathe in while shifting back slightly and transferring your weight to your left heel.
3. For a *four-step approach,* exhale slowly and transfer your weight to the ball of your right foot. As your weight becomes centered on the ball of your right foot, take your first step with your left foot as you move your ball into the push-away.

   For a *five-step approach,* exhale slowly while you slide your right foot forward into the baby step. *Do not move your ball as you take this sliding baby step.* Then take your second step with your left foot while moving the bowling ball into the push-away.
4. Repeat this drill five times without holding anything in your hand. Then repeat it five more times while holding your bowling ball. If you don't have a bowling ball, use an object that simulates a bowling ball, such as an iron.

Assessment 4-2

Weight Transfer Drill

Name _____ Section _____ Date _____

To perform this drill, you will need the following equipment:
- A full-length mirror

For best results, perform this drill 10 times per day for 3 weeks.

1. Line up so that the bowling side of your body faces a full-length mirror.
2. Take your stance position.
3. Inhale slowly, relax, and then exhale slowly.
4. Transfer the weight of your lower body from your right heel to the ball of your left foot. (For left-handers, do the opposite.)

Assessment 4-3

Name _____ Section _____ Date _____

To perform this drill, you will again need the following equipment:
- A full-length mirror
- A bowling ball

For best results, perform this drill 10 times per day for 3 weeks.

1. Line up so that the bowling side of your body faces the full-length mirror.
2. While holding the bowling ball, take your stance position.
3. Inhale slowly, relax, and then exhale slowly.
4. Go through each step of your approach, one step at a time. After each step, take a couple of slow breaths, holding them in for a few moments. After breathing, look at your reflection in the mirror. Where is the ball located? What is the posture of your upper torso, knees, and hips?
5. Before going to the next step, rock forward and then backward. Feel the point where you are best balanced.
6. Evaluate your finish position using the criteria presented in step 4.

Assessment 4-4

Name _____ Section _____ Date _____

Take this approach checklist with you whenever you bowl. Use it to evaluate your progress. For best results concentrate on a portion of the checklist, such as the four-step approach, and work on it until you feel it begin to flow. Then move on to the armswing, the release, and so on. Your ultimate reward will be successful bowling.

Two approach checklists are provided: one for right-handers and one for left-handers.

RIGHT-HANDED BOWLER'S APPROACH CHECKLIST

1. Alignment
   - _____ Maintain the "line in your mind" at all times
   - _____ Make sure you start and finish on the same board
   - _____ Three-foot arrow from the right shoulder lined up with target line
   - _____ Eyes focused on target
2. Balance
   - _____ Body weight is slightly forward on balls of feet
   - _____ Knees bent at 20-degree angle
   - _____ Spine inclined forward 15 degrees
   - _____ Keep bowling arm out 2 inches in backswing and in 2 inches in forward swing
   - _____ Use left arm as stabilizer for left-to-right balance
3. Synchronization (four-step approach)
   - _____ Feet and bowling arm work in unison
   - _____ Right arm moves with toe of right foot during first two steps
   - _____ Right arm moves with left heel during last two steps
4. Four-step approach
   Step 1
   - _____ Right arm and right foot move as one
   - _____ Right hand ends up positioned down and above right toe
   - _____ Elbow remains bent
   - _____ Left hand remains on left side of ball
   - _____ Right forearm lined up with target line
   Step 2
   - _____ Left foot moves forward
   - _____ Left hand leaves ball and begins to move forward and left
   - _____ Right arm arcs downward and back
   - _____ Elbow fully straightened by end of second step

65

_____ At end of second step, ball at lowest point of backswing, perpendicular to the floor

Step 3

_____ Right foot moves forward

_____ Right arm arcs back, completes backswing

_____ At highest point, armswing 3 to 4 inches above shoulder

_____ Elbow remains straight throughout step

Step 4

_____ Left foot moves forward

_____ Right arm lined up with left heel

_____ Right arm ends up pointed down toward floor

_____ Knees bend an additional 3 to 4 inches

_____ Bowling arm kept close to body

_____ Right hip moves in slightly

_____ Right foot slides sideways, crossing back of left foot

_____ Left arm moves back toward body

5. Release

_____ Thumb releases during slide of fourth step

_____ Counterclockwise wrist, hand, and finger rotation to 10-o'clock thumb position

_____ Lift action, not arm extension

_____ Fingers release

_____ Left arm moves back to left pants pocket

6. Finish position

_____ Follow through up with right arm

_____ Right leg remains slid in back of body, crossing left leg

_____ Left arm out from body and lined up with left pants pocket

_____ Eyes remain fixed on target line

7. Armswing

_____ Armswing never changes

_____ Maintain correct swing

8. Armswing tempo

_____ Synchronized with foot tempo

_____ Adjust by adjusting ball height in stance

_____ Fast: at waist height or below

_____ Medium: at waist height

_____ Slow: at chest height

_____ Changes in tempo during armswing

_____ Fast at beginning

_____ More relaxed during approach

_____ Aggressive lifting action during release and follow-through

LEFT-HANDED BOWLER'S APPROACH CHECKLIST

Name _____   Section _____   Date _____

1. Alignment
   _____ Maintain the "line in your mind" at all times
   _____ Make sure you start and finish on the same board
   _____ Three-foot arrow from the left shoulder lined up with target line
   _____ Eyes focused on target
2. Balance
   _____ Body weight is slightly forward on balls of feet
   _____ Knees bent at 20-degree angle
   _____ Spine inclined forward 15 degrees
   _____ Keep bowling arm out 2 inches in backswing and in 2 inches in forward swing
   _____ Use right arm as stabilizer for left-to-right balance
3. Synchronization (four-step approach)
   _____ Feet and bowling arm work in unison
   _____ Left arm moves with toe of left foot during first two steps
   _____ Left arm moves with right heel during last two steps
4. Four-step approach
   Step 1
   _____ Left arm and left foot move as one
   _____ Left hand ends up positioned down and above left toe
   _____ Elbow remains bent
   _____ Right hand remains on right side of ball
   _____ Left forearm lined up with target line
   Step 2
   _____ Right foot moves forward
   _____ Right hand leaves ball and begins to move forward and right
   _____ Left arm arcs downward and back
   _____ Elbow fully straightened by end of second step
   _____ At end of second step, ball at lowest point of backswing, perpendicular to the floor
   Step 3
   _____ Left foot moves forward
   _____ Left arm arcs back, completes backswing
   _____ At highest point, armswing 3 to 4 inches above shoulder
   _____ Elbow remains straight throughout step
   Step 4
   _____ Right foot moves forward
   _____ Left arm lined up with right heel
   _____ Left arm ends up pointed down toward floor
   _____ Knees bend an additional 3 to 4 inches
   _____ Bowling arm kept close to body
   _____ Left hip moves in slightly

_____ Left foot slides sideways, crossing back of right foot
_____ Right arm moves back toward body
5. Release
_____ Thumb releases during slide of fourth step
_____ Clockwise wrist, hand, and finger rotation to 2-o'clock thumb position
_____ Lift action, not arm extension
_____ Fingers release
_____ Right arm moves back to right pants pocket
6. Finish position
_____ Follow through up with left arm
_____ Left leg remains slid in back of body, crossing right leg
_____ Right arm out from body and lined up with right pants pocket
_____ Eyes remain fixed on target line
7. Armswing
_____ Armswing never changes
_____ Maintain correct swing
8. Armswing tempo
_____ Synchronized with foot tempo
_____ Adjust by adjusting ball height in stance
    _____ Fast: at waist height or below
    _____ Medium: at waist height
    _____ Slow: at chest height
_____ Changes in tempo during armswing
    _____ Fast at beginning
    _____ More relaxed during approach
    _____ Aggressive lifting action during release and follow-through

CHAPTER 5

FOCUS ON POSITION: ARMSWING, RELEASE, AND FINISH

OBJECTIVES

After reading this chapter, you should be able to do the following:

- Describe and explain the armswing.
- Describe and explain the release.
- Describe and explain the finish position.
- Demonstrate a proper armswing technique.
- Demonstrate a proper release technique.

KEY TERMS

While reading this chapter, you will become familiar with the following terms:

► Backswing

► Backup Ball

► Delivery

► Forward Swing

► Pro Groove

► Push-Away

► Reverse Curve

ARMSWING

This chapter analyzes the armswing from two views: front-to-back and side. From the front-to-back perspective, the chapter will show you how to maintain your armswing in a narrow **pro groove.** The side view will show you how to develop a consistently smooth pendulum swing.

Armswing equates to accuracy. Keeping your arm on line and developing a consistent armswing are the two keys to bowling accuracy. You must learn to develop consistency in your game, and a consistent armswing is more important than any other area of bowling. The information in the accompanying box will help you remember to keep your armswing consistent.

FRONT-TO-BACK PERSPECTIVE

To visualize the front-to-back perspective, imagine that you are standing inside the face of a clock, as Figure 5-1 shows. In this mental picture you are facing the 12-o'clock position. Just to your right is the 1-o'clock position. Directly behind you is the 6-o'clock position, and just to the right of this is the 5-o'clock position.

If you bowl right-handed, during the armswing you want to do the following:

1. Push the ball out between 12 and 1 o'clock during the **push-away.**
2. Arc the ball back between 5 and 6 o'clock during the **backswing.**
3. Arc the ball forward between 12 and 1 o'clock during the **forward swing** and de-**livery.**

FIGURE 5-1 Armswing: a front-to-back perspective.

Performance Tip

Never Vary Your Armswing

Where you line up in the stance will vary. How you hold the bowling ball may vary; but your armswing should *never* vary.

Figure 5-2 shows these steps for a right-handed bowler.

If you bowl left-handed, you want to do the following:

1. Push the ball out between 12 and 11 o'clock during the push-away.
2. Arc the ball back between 7 and 6 o'clock during the backswing.
3. Arc the ball forward between 12 and 11 o'clock during the forward swing and delivery.

Figure 5-3 shows these steps for a left-handed bowler.

► Stay Inside the Pro Groove

Note that there is a slight looping action during the armswing. The emphasis here is that the motion is slight—no more than 2 inches either way. This narrow 4-inch slot is called the pro groove. Keep your armswing inside the pro groove to achieve consistent accuracy.

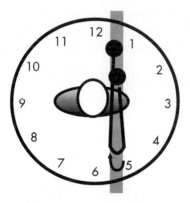

FIGURE 5-2 Right-handed armswing.

FIGURE 5-3 Left-handed armswing.

► Pro Groove

A 4-inch wide area describing the path of a bowler's armswing as it passes from back to front. Bowlers who keep their arm inside this narrow "groove" achieve high accuracy.

► Push-Away

A bowler's arm motion as the approach begins; moving the ball out and down.

► Backswing

The backward arm motion made during the approach, beginning after the push-away and ending when the arm reaches its maximum travel behind the bowler or at the top of the backswing.

► Forward Swing

The forward arm motion made during the approach, beginning at the end of the backswing and ending when the ball is released.

► Delivery

The overall motion a bowler makes beginning with the push-away and ending with the release and follow-through.

Take some time to observe other bowlers the next time you visit a bowling center. You will note that some bowlers tend to wrap their bowling arm in back of them during the backswing. When they do this, you will see that the ball will go out to the right (if the bowler you are watching is right-handed). You can use this observation to your advantage. If you note that *your* ball is going out to the right, you are probably doing the same thing that the person you observed was doing. Figure 5-4 gives a description of this armswing problem.

Other bowlers let the ball bounce out and away from them in the backswing. This makes the ball go in to the left (if the bowler you are watching is right-handed). When you bowl and note that your ball is going to the left, you reasonably assume that you too are letting the ball bounce out and away from you. Figure 5-5 gives a description of this armswing problem.

▶ Watch That First Step!

An inaccurate armswing is often caused by pushing the ball to the right or left as you take the first step of your approach. Push the ball out straight and down toward your right foot (or left foot if you bowl left-handed) during that first step. If you do this, you are getting off to a good, straight start.

Improper timing can also throw your armswing off. The box on p. 73 contains some points to remember.

SIDE PERSPECTIVE

Figure 5-6 shows the armswing from a side perspective. Note that all footsteps are numbered to show how the movements of your feet correspond to a properly timed armswing. Note also that the backswing goes up to about shoulder height. It is important to keep the height of your armswing consistent to promote consistent timing.

FIGURE 5-4 Armswing troubleshooting tip 1: Arm in = ball out.

FIGURE 5-5 Armswing troubleshooting tip 2: Arm out = ball in.

Performance Tip

Points to Remember About the Armswing

- If your armswing is faster than your feet, the ball will go in. This is because your arm reaches the release point before your feet and closes your shoulders relative to the lane.

- If your armswing is slower than your feet, the ball will go out. This is because your feet reach the release point before your arm and open your shoulders relative to the lane.

- Make sure your foot and arm move together during the first step. You may want to experiment with raising or lowering the ball in the stance to correct these timing problems.

First three steps = Backswing

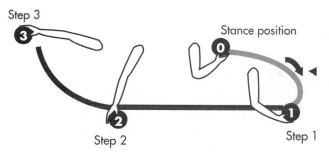

Fourth step = Delivery swing

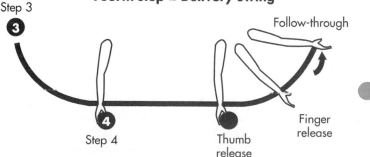

FIGURE 5-6 Armswing: a side perspective.

As you reach the end of the backswing and begin the forward swing, your arm arcs down toward the floor and then back up to the finish position. To better visualize this, imagine an airplane coming in for a landing and then taking off again just before it touches the ground. The arc that the plane described is what a proper forward swing resembles.

Figure 5-6 also shows the points where your thumb and fingers release the ball. Your thumb releases at the lowest point of the forward swing, just after the fourth step. Your fingers release as you begin arcing up toward the finish position. Since your fingers are on the side of the ball, they impart sideways spin on the ball, which gives it the potential to hook as it travels down the lane.

RELEASE

Beginning bowlers often have difficulty with the release. Perhaps this is because there are different types of releases. A beginning bowler will often become confused or try to adopt more advanced releases before mastering the simple ones.

Beginning bowlers sometimes fear that they will drop the ball prematurely. However, the forward momentum of the bowling ball usually keeps it firmly against the hand until it is time to release it.

When performed properly, the release occurs naturally. The holes in a bowling ball are drilled to cause your thumb and fingers to drop out of the ball at the proper time.

As a beginner you should concentrate on two simple release techniques: the suitcase release and the straight ball release. Let's examine them in detail.

SUITCASE RELEASE

The suitcase release was explained in Chapter 4. Here's how to perform it. Put your thumb in the 10-o'clock "handshake" position. Then maintain this position throughout your approach and release.

If you bowl left-handed, put your thumb in the 2-o'clock position and maintain it throughout your approach and release.

Figure 5-7 shows these positions for right- and left-handed bowlers.

To perform a proper suitcase release, it helps to develop a mental picture of reaching out and shaking hands with the second target arrow. By doing so, your thumb should stay in the correct position.

▶ Release Timing

If you hold the ball naturally and your thumb and fingers fit comfortably in the holes (not too tight or not too loose), your thumb should drop out of the ball at the end of your fourth step. This is the lowest part of your forward swing.

After your thumb drops out, your fingers remain in the ball as you continue your forward swing, lifting up and out toward the finish position. Since your fingers are on the side of the ball, this natural lifting action imparts sideways spin on the ball. Under medium lane conditions (not very oily or very dry), the ball's spinning action will cause it to hook into the strike pocket. Figure 5-8 shows the release.

Left-handed bowler   Right-handed bowler

FIGURE 5-7 Suitcase release *(back view)*.

FIGURE 5-8 Release.

▶ Maintain Your Hand Position

Observe bowlers at the bowling center again. You will note that some bowlers try to force the ball to hook by turning their hand up over the ball at the moment of release. Although this technique may work some of the time, it does not promote consistency. It is important to maintain the same hand position from the moment you line up in the stance until you end up in the finish position.

There is no need to flip the ball and force it to hook. Always remember that the action of your fingers lifting on the side of the ball imparts the *natural* sideways spin necessary for the hook. The accompanying box contains information you should know before deciding to change your release style.

▶ Beware of Backup Ball

Some bowlers have problems with a **backup ball** or **reverse curve.** A backup ball ends up curving away from the center head pin and toward the channel, as shown in Figure 5-9.

A backup ball occurs because the bowler's thumb opens out during the release. The weight of the ball sometimes causes the bowler to flop the hand open, making the thumb flip out and away from the bowler instead of pointing down toward the 10-o'clock position.

Some bowlers compensate for a backup ball by lining up differently in the stance and angling their shoulders relative to the lane. This movement only partially corrects the problem. Even if the backup ball hits the strike pocket, the improper angle of the shot usually results in a low percentage of strikes. The tips in the box on p. 78 may help in correcting a backup ball.

Performance Tip

Advanced Releases Are for Advanced Bowlers!

Although there are some advanced releases that involve cocking the hand in the stance and then uncocking it during the release, these releases are best left to experienced bowlers who have mastered the basics.

▶ Backup Ball

A ball that ends up curving away from the center head pin and toward the right channel for right-handers (opposite direction for left-handers). Sometimes referred to as a reverse curve.

▶ Reverse Curve

See Backup Ball.

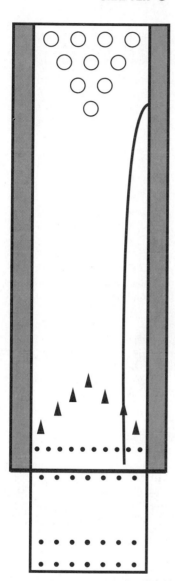

FIGURE 5-9 A backup ball's path.

Figure 5-10 shows this technique for right- and left-handed bowlers.

▶ Maintain Your Wrist Position

Do you remember the three wrist positions that were explained previously: cupped, straight, and broken? To refresh your memory, see Figure 5-11.

Although any of these positions is acceptable, a beginner should always use the straight wrist position because it is easiest to maintain. Remember—whatever wrist position you start with, maintain it throughout your stance, approach, release, and follow-through.

STRAIGHT BALL RELEASE

Although the suitcase release is probably the best for you as a beginner, the straight ball release is good for certain situations. For example, if the lanes are very oily and your ball won't hook (or the lanes are very dry and your ball hooks too much), you want to try to roll a straighter ball. You will also discover that a straight ball is great for making difficult spares where accuracy is critical. To perform a straight ball release, point your thumb straight up toward the ceiling (12-o'clock position) in the stance. Maintain this position throughout your approach, release, and finish position. Figure 5-12 illustrates your thumb position when the ball is released.

During the slide your thumb should release from the ball first. As your fingers slide out and up, the ball will simply roll from your fingers and onto the lane. This promotes a good rolling action on the lane and virtually no spin is imparted. The box on p. 79 provides a tip on lining up for a straight ball release.

You will find that a straight ball release produces greater accuracy than a suitcase release, but keep in mind that a straight ball doesn't produce as high a percentage of strikes. This is because the ball doesn't hook and therefore doesn't hit the strike pocket at the proper angle.

Performance Tip

Eliminating the Backup Ball

- If you experience problems with a backup ball, remember to keep your thumb pointed toward your pants pocket throughout your approach and release.

- If you try to maintain your thumb position but still experience problems with a backup ball, try the "I changed my mind" method. Line up with your thumb open and out if you want. Then, right at the moment when your thumb releases, change your mind and flip your thumb back toward your pants pocket.

Line up in stance with thumb in 1:00 position

At moment of thumb release, "change your mind": flip thumbhole to 10:00 position

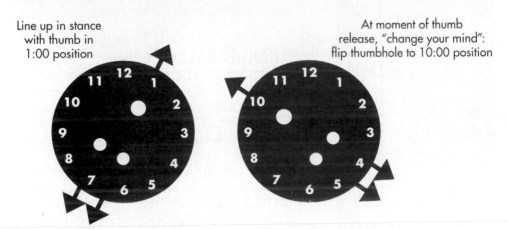

Right-handed bowler

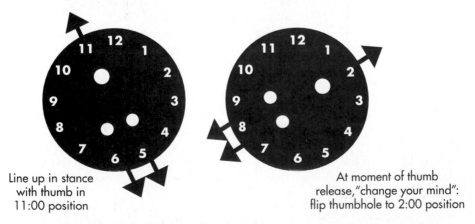

Line up in stance with thumb in 11:00 position

At moment of thumb release, "change your mind": flip thumbhole to 2:00 position

Left-handed bowler

FIGURE 5-10 "I changed my mind" technique *(back view)*.

Performance Tip

How to Line Up for a Straight Ball Release

Since a straight ball doesn't hook to any great extent, right-handed bowlers should line up a few boards farther to the right in the stance than they normally do. Left-handed bowlers should line up a few boards farther to the left.

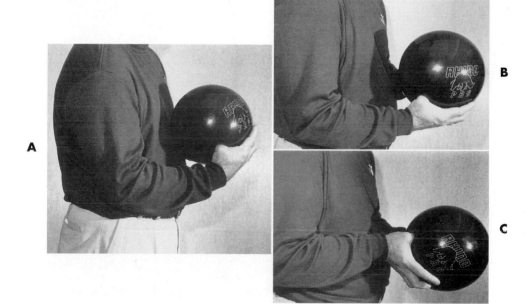

FIGURE 5-11 **A,** Cupped, **B,** straight, and **C,** broken wrist positions.

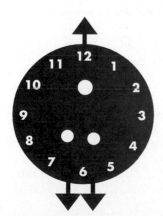

FIGURE 5-12 Ball position for a straight ball release.

FINISH POSITION

Many bowlers fail to understand the importance of the finish position. After all, the ball has already been released and is on its way down the lane. They think that there is nothing more they can do to influence the outcome of their shot. The finish position is important because it promotes a correct follow-through.

Imagine that you are a quarterback throwing a pass. If your hands stopped at the moment you released the football, speed, accuracy, and distance would be sacrificed. Keeping this in mind, what would happen if a tennis player's hand stopped the instant after connecting? The tennis ball probably wouldn't clear the net. In bowling, correct follow-through and finish position are just as important for the same reason as for the quarterback and tennis player: they help maintain accuracy, body balance, and consistency.

COMPONENTS

The finish position has two components: the slide and the follow-through.

▶ Slide

At the end of the fourth step of your approach, your left foot "plants" for the slide. At the same time, your right foot begins to slide sideways in back of your body. If you are left-handed, the opposite is true; your right foot plants, and your left foot begins its sideways slide.

Moving your foot in back of your body accomplishes three things:
1. It helps move your hip inside to allow more clearance for the bowling ball to move past.
2. It provides a broader base to promote better balance during the release and follow-through.
3. It shifts your weight toward the side opposite the bowling ball, thus creating better balance.

Remember to flex your knees a little more during the slide. This promotes better ball delivery onto the lane and contributes to better balance.

▶ Follow-Through

Two main points are important to remember during the follow-through:
1. Lift your arm out and up.
2. Keep your body down.

As the ball rolls from your fingers, your arm should continue to arc up toward the ceiling. Also, your hand should remain aligned with the target line that the ball follows down the lane. For example, if you were rolling a strike ball, your hand would be pointed at the second target arrow.

At the same time you should keep your hips low. This does not mean to bend over from the waist but to lower your hips and keep them low as your arm goes up

FIGURE 5-13 Body position at the end of the follow-through.

toward the ceiling. When you perform this motion properly, it feels comfortable, like sitting back in a chair. Just keep your spine tilted 15 degrees forward, flex your knees, and let the ball roll right off your fingers as you lift your arm up toward the ceiling. Figure 5-13 shows how you should be positioned at the end of the follow-through.

SIDE PERSPECTIVE

Examine Figure 5-13, which shows a side view of the finish position. In the

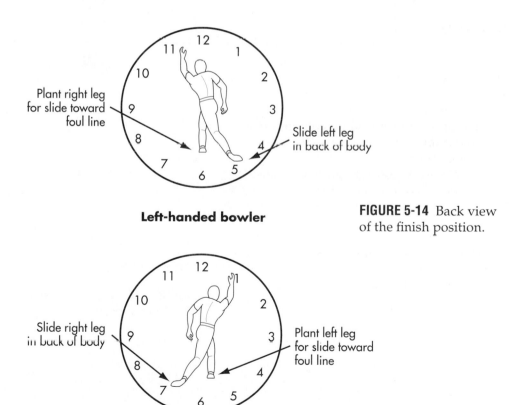

Plant right leg for slide toward foul line

Slide left leg in back of body

Left-handed bowler

FIGURE 5-14 Back view of the finish position.

Slide right leg in back of body

Plant left leg for slide toward foul line

Right-handed bowler

perfect finish position your head, knee, and toe should be in a straight line perpendicular to the floor. Note the following:
- The bowler's arm has continued arcing upward after ball release.
- The bowler's spine is at the same angle as it was in the stance.
- The bowler's knees have flexed further to complement a better delivery of the ball onto the lane.

BACK-TO-FRONT PERSPECTIVE

Now look at Figure 5-14, which shows a back-to-front perspective of the finish position for right- and left-handed bowlers.

A right-handed bowler's right arm should end up approximately at the 1-o'clock position with the left leg at 6 o'clock. The right leg is at 7 o'clock, and the head is at 12 o'clock.

A left-handed bowler's left arm should end up at approximately the 11-o'clock position with the right leg at 6 o'clock. The left leg is at 5 o'clock, and the head is at 12 o'clock.

SUMMARY

- A consistent armswing equates to bowling accuracy.
- When performed properly, the release occurs naturally.
- Beginning bowlers should concentrate on two release techniques: the suitcase release and the straight ball release.
- The finish position is important because it promotes a correct follow-through.

• • •

You can use the following assessment activities to develop and hone your armswing, release, and finish position. The first practice drill, for your armswing, can be done at home. The practice drills for the release and finish position should be done at a bowling center.

FIGURE 5-15 Side perspective of the finish position.

Assessment 5-1

At-Home Practice Drill for the Armswing

Name   Section   Date

You can improve your armswing technique if you do this at-home practice drill. If you do the drill three times each week for at least 4 weeks, you will note a pronounced improvement in your armswing and game. To do this drill, you need the following equipment:

- A full-length mirror
- A roll of masking tape
- An object you can use to simulate a bowling ball and grip well, such as an iron

1. Attach a piece of masking tape vertically down the center of a full-length mirror.
2. Face the mirror and line up your shoulder with the tape.
3. Practice your armswing. Try to keep your arm and hand lined up with the tape so that they do not deviate more than 2 inches to either side of the tape.
4. Practice this 10 times, and then line up so that you are six or seven steps away from the mirror.
5. Practice your armswing while doing your approach toward the mirror. Try to maintain the same 2-inch deviation. Practice this 10 times.

Assessment 5-2

Bowling Center Practice Drill for the Release

_____   _____   _____
Name   Section   Date

You can perform this practice drill at the bowling center to analyze your release. This drill covers four factors that you can control to fine-tune your release: timing, wrist position, elbow position, and hand/ball position.

1. Select one of these factors, and experiment with it for a couple weeks. Watch how your adjustments affect the behavior of your ball on the lane.
2. Now select another factor, and work on it until you feel comfortable.
3. After you feel confident in your ability to make these adjustments, try combining the factors, one at a time, until you have combined all four and have fine-tuned your style.

Assessment 5-3

Bowling Center Practice Drill for the Finish Position

Name _____ Section _____ Date _____

Here's a practice drill you can do at the bowling center that will help you attain a winning finish position. You need a camera and the help of a friend to perform this drill.

1. While bowling, have a friend take side and back view photographs of you in your finish position. You can also have a videotape shot; many bowling centers provide this service for a small fee.

2. Compare the photographs to the illustrations in this text. Ask yourself the following questions:
   a. Are there any indications that my timing may be too late or too early?
   b. Am I in a position for maximum balance and power?

3. Isolate the areas you need to work on, and practice perfecting your finish position.

4. After a few weeks, have your friend take photographs again.

5. Compare the photographs to the illustrations in this text again. Ask yourself the following questions:
   a. Where have I improved?
   b. Have my scores improved?
   c. What do I still need to work on?

6. Repeat the procedure until you master the secrets of a winning finish position.

CHAPTER 6

PUTTING IT ALL TOGETHER:
STRIKES AND SPARES

OBJECTIVES

After reading this chapter, you should be able to do the following:

- Refresh your knowledge of lane basics.
- Explain the theory for making a strike.
- Explain the methods used to make a spare.
- Define and explain the term *math bowling.*
- Explain how to adjust to varying lane conditions.

KEY TERMS

While reading this chapter, you will become familiar with the following terms:

- ▶ Baby Split
- ▶ Dialed In
- ▶ Hard Pocket Hit
- ▶ Key Pin Positions
- ▶ Math Bowling
- ▶ Soft Pocket Hit
- ▶ Split
- ▶ Strike Pocket

LANE BASICS: A REFRESHER

Even though you have previously learned about lanes, it's a good idea to refresh your memory before we begin explaining the process of making strikes and converting spares.

Remember the following:

- All lanes are created equal. *Every lane in the world is the same length and width.* The boards are spaced the same distance apart (about 1 inch), and the locator dots and target arrows are always in the same place.
- There are three sets of locator dots in front of the foul line.
- Each dot is spaced five boards from the next, and all three sets line up with each other, as shown in Figure 6-1.
- There is also a set of locator dots beyond the foul line that do not line up with the three sets beyond the foul line. The dots after the foul line are used by advanced bowlers as "rear gun sights." Don't worry about them now.
- The seven target arrows out on the lane are 15 feet from the foul line. The arrows on the right side are for right-handed bowlers, and the arrows on the left side are for left-handed bowlers, as shown in Figure 6-2.
- The target arrows are numbered right to left for right-handed bowlers and left to right for left-handed bowlers.
- Use the second and third sets of target arrows to aim your shot.
- The target arrows are in line with the locator dots.

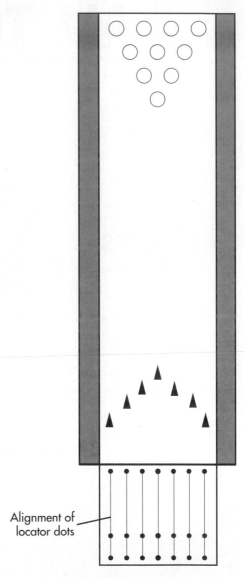

FIGURE 6-1 Locator dots.

- The center locator dot corresponds with the center target arrow and so on. Figure 6-2 also illustrates the locator dot–to–target arrow alignment.

- The locator dots and target arrows form a line to the outside pins. Figure 6-3 illustrates this alignment.
- The outside pins are the seven pins forming the V that is pointing toward you. These pins are referred to as the **key pin positions** and are shown in Figure 6-4. Any spare can be made by simply aiming at one of the seven key pin positions.
- There are 10 pins, each having a number, in the pin triangle. The pins are numbered according to Figure 6-5. The key pin positions are shaded.

To remember the pin numbering scheme, start with the head pin as #1 and then count from left to right. In the rest of this chapter, pins will be identified by their number.

The key to making strikes and spares depends on how effectively you use the target arrows as an aiming aid. Remember that the target arrows mirror the location of the key pin positions. Remember also that the pins are 60 feet away from you and the target arrows are only 15 feet away. It is much easier to aim for a target 15 feet away as opposed to 60 feet away.

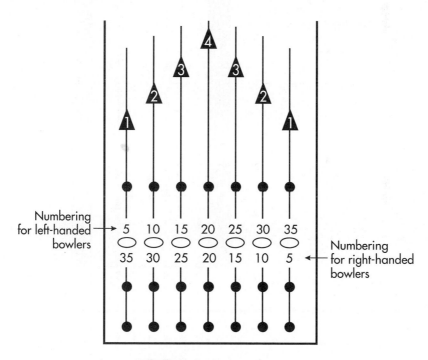

FIGURE **6-2** Target arrows.

▶ **Key Pin Positions**
Seven pins forming the V that is pointing toward you as you look at them from the approach.

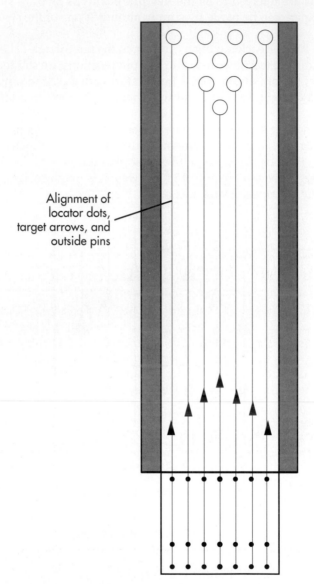

Alignment of locator dots, target arrows, and outside pins

FIGURE 6-3 Relationship of locator dots and target arrows to the pins.

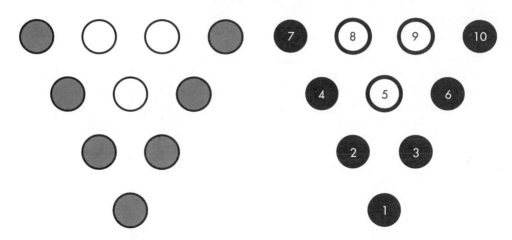

FIGURE 6-4 Seven key pin positions.

FIGURE 6-5 Pin triangle and pin numbering scheme.

MAKING STRIKES: GOAL OF THE GAME

The object of bowling is to knock down as many pins as you can, so your goal for each game should be to make as many strikes as you can. Making a strike does not just happen; it requires your utmost concentration and ability to get in a proper stance and execute a near-perfect approach, armswing, release, and follow-through. Always use a hook ball on your strike shot like the pros do. A hook creates maximum pin action.

BALL SPEED IS CRITICAL

It is also important to have good ball speed to create pin action. Pin action causes the pins to bounce off each other as they fall and more pins fall. If you use a hook release and the ball enters the **strike pocket** at the proper angle and speed, the ball hits only the #1, #3, #5, and #9 pins. The strike pocket is an area in the pin triangle between the #1 and #3 pins for right-handed bowlers and between the #1 and #2 pins for left-handed bowlers. The rest of the pins are knocked down by the domino effect of these pins bouncing off the other pins (pin action).

▶ **Strike Pocket**
Area in the pin triangle between the #1 and #3 pins for right-handed bowlers and between the #1 and #2 pins for left-handed bowlers.

EFFECTS OF HOOK

If your ball doesn't hook enough, it enters the strike pocket but leaves the #5 or #10 pin standing. This is known as a **soft pocket hit,** the effects of which are shown in Figure 6-6.

Conversely, if your ball hooks too much, it leaves the #4 pin standing, or you may even end up with a 4-9 split. A **split** occurs when two or more pins are left standing and they are separated by at least one pin position. The reason for this is because the ball is snapping and hooking too sharply as it enters the strike pocket, diminishing pin action. This is known as a **hard pocket hit,** the effects of which are shown in Figure 6-7.

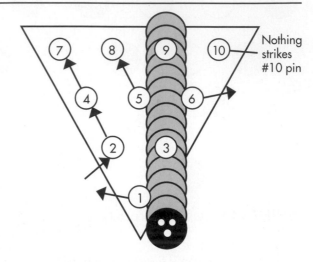

FIGURE 6-6 Effects of a soft pocket hit.

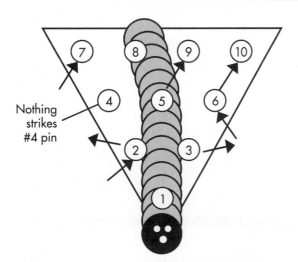

FIGURE 6-7 Effects of a hard pocket hit.

▶ **Soft Pocket Hit**
Action a ball makes as it enters the pin triangle when its rotation has diminished because it is too slow. Even though the ball enters the strike pocket, a strike usually does not occur.

▶ **Split**
Situation in which there is a gap between the pins left standing after your first shot.

▶ **Hard Pocket Hit**
Action a ball makes as it enters the pin triangle when its rotation is excessive because it is too fast and curving sharply. Although the ball enters the strike pocket, a strike usually does not occur.

MAKING SPARES: NEXT BEST GOAL

When your first shot doesn't produce a strike (and many of them won't), don't worry; go to plan B: make a spare. Making spares is the way to increase your score faster than anything else. The quickest way for you to bowl games in excess of 170 is to make all the spares. In bowling, making a spare is called a spare conversion.

Your strategy changes when attempting to convert a spare. Earlier we made the point that you should always throw a hook ball on your strike shot. When making spares, you want to achieve greater ball control and accuracy to make the ball enter the location for which you aimed. You achieve control in this situation by throwing a straight ball.

THROWING A STRAIGHT BALL

Let's quickly review how to throw a straight ball. Get in the stance, and hold your ball so that your thumb is up at the 12-o'clock position. Keep it in that position as you execute your approach, armswing, release, and follow-through. When you release the ball, your thumb should be locked in the 12-o'clock position. If you have executed the release properly, the ball's path to the pins will be straight.

Remember also to keep your shoulders lined up. Keep the "line in your mind" and the imaginary 3-foot arrow off your shoulders we discussed in Chapter 5. To make spares on the left side of the pin triangle, move to the right on your approach and turn your shoulder in toward the pin. On spares to the right, move left on your approach and turn your shoulder out away from the pin. The accompanying box summarizes key points to remember for making spares.

Performance Tip

Making Spares: Things to Keep in Mind

If you keep the line in your mind, your shoulders lined up, and your thumb at the 12-o'clock position when you take your shot, you will convert the spare every time!

MATH BOWLING

The art of converting spares is often called **math bowling.** Although this term may seem imposing, the only math you need to know is simple addition and subtraction. Actually, making spares is as easy as 1-2-3.

1. Determine which key pin position to hit to make the spare.
2. Line up your feet in the proper position *mathematically* by moving right or left the proper number of boards.
3. Aim for the correct target.

The next two sections of this chapter discuss making spares for right- or left-handed bowlers, beginning with right-handed bowlers. If you are a left-handed bowler, you may skip this section and go to the section entitled "Making Spares: Left-Handed Bowlers" (p. 104).

MAKING SPARES: RIGHT-HANDED BOWLERS

STEP 1: DETERMINE KEY PIN POSITION

There are literally hundreds of possible spare conversion combinations you might be faced with in any given game. Does this mean that you need to memorize hundreds of different shots? No, it is much less overwhelming if you look at each shot as a one-pin shot and remember that you can convert any spare by aiming for the proper key pin position. A few examples will make this point.

▶ Example 1: 4-7 Shot

A common spare is the 4-7. By this we mean that the #4 and #7 pins are standing after your first shot. To make this shot aim for the #4 pin. If you aimed correctly, the ball will knock the #4 pin into the #7 pin and knock it down. It's a domino effect that Figure 6-8 shows.

▶ Example 2: No Key Pins Left Standing

Sometimes no key pins are left standing. When this is the case, you perform what is known as a *make-believe shot.* In other words, you aim for a point where a key position pin would be standing.

▶ **Math Bowling**

Process of adding or subtracting the number of boards from the board you would normally position yourself for a strike shot (initial position). When you make this calculation, you adjust your stance to that board for your second shot.

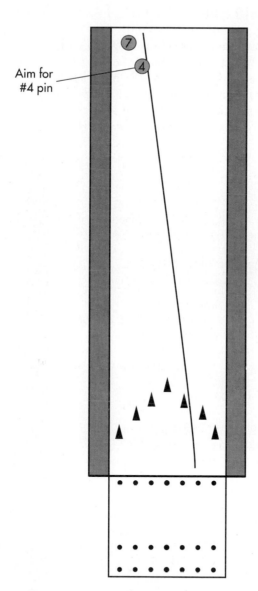

Aim for
#4 pin

FIGURE 6-8 Converting the 4-7 for right-handed bowlers: aim for the pin that is closest to you.

Assume that your first shot knocked down all the pins but the #5 pin. What key pin would you aim for? The #1 or head pin. Figure 6-9 shows this make-believe shot.

▶ Example 3: 3-10 Split

Another common spare is the 3-10 split (the #3 and #10 pins are left standing). This combination is called a split because there is a gap between the pins, as shown in Figure 6-10. This is also an example of a **baby split.**

In this example, *do not* aim for either the #3 or the #10 pin. If you did hit one, the other would remain standing. Instead, aim between them, or where the #6 key position pin would have been standing. Figure 6-11 shows how this split is converted.

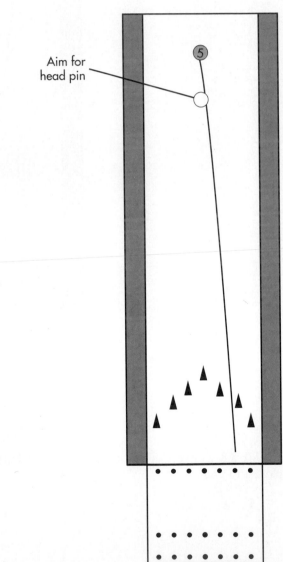

FIGURE 6-9 Make-believe shot for right-handed bowlers.

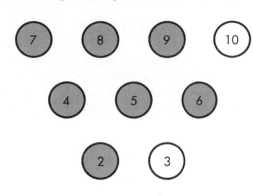

FIGURE 6-10 The 3-10 split.

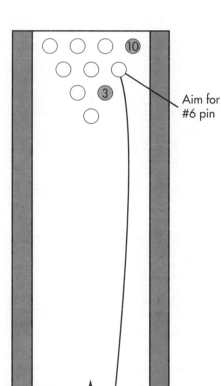

Aim for
#6 pin

FIGURE 6-11 Converting the 3-10 split for
right-handed bowlers.

▶ **Baby Split**
Split with a gap between the pins that is
such that a bowling ball passing between
the pins would knock them down. To
make a baby split, your ball must pass
between the pins.

STEP 2: ALIGN YOUR FEET

The next step is to move either right or left of where you line up for a strike shot. For shots to the right of the #1 (head) pin, move to the left. For shots to the left of the #1 (head) pin, move to the right. When making #1 or #5 pin spares, don't move either right or left; stay in your strike position.

▶ Shots to Right of Head Pin

For shots to the right of the head pin, move your stance position left four boards at a time; in other words:
- For #3 pin spares, move left four boards from where you line up for a strike.
- For #6 pin spares, move left eight boards.
- For #10 spares, move left 12 boards.

▶ Shots to Left of Head Pin

For shots to the left of the head pin, move your stance position right three boards at a time.
- For #2 pin spares, move right three boards from your line-up for a strike.
- For #4 pin spares, move right six boards.
- For #7 pin spares, move right nine boards.

By now you must be asking the question, "Why four boards for shots to the right and three boards for shots to the left?" Here's why. You are throwing against the rotation of the ball when you make spares to the right and with the rotation of the ball when you make spares to the left. The one-board difference counteracts the ball's rotational effect.

STEP 3: ALIGN YOUR TARGET

When you attempt to make a strike, you should aim for the second target arrow, but this rule changes when you are lining up to make a spare. As you shift over in the stance to make the spare, the target arrow you aim for will also change. Sometimes you will be aiming between the target arrows. The following pointers will help you decide where to aim to convert a spare:
- For #1 and #5 pin spares, do not change your target. Aim for the second target arrow as you would for a strike.
- For all spares to the left of the #1 pin (head pin), aim between the second and third target arrows.
- For #6 and #10 pin spares, aim at the third target arrow.

SHOULDER ALIGNMENT WHEN MAKING SPARES

As your position in the stance and your target change, so will the angle of your body relative to the lane.

Remember the discussion in Chapter 5 about how your shoulders could either be opened, closed, or straight relative to the lane? It was also mentioned that for strike shots, your shoulders should be straight relative to the lane.

When you attempt to convert a spare, the above is not always true. What is true in this case is that you should always point your body in the direction of the target. We call this *presetting the angle of the shoulders.* To determine how to position your shoulders, remember these rules.

- When making #1 and #5 position spares, keep your shoulders straight relative to the lane, just as you would when making a strike. Figure 6-12 shows how your shoulders should be aligned for this shot.
- When making shots to the right of the head pin, open your shoulders relative to the lane. Figure 6-13 shows how your shoulders should be aligned for these shots.
- When making shots to the left of the head pin, close your shoulders relative to the lane. Figure 6-14 shows how your shoulders should be aligned for these shots.

WALK STRAIGHT TO FOUL LINE

Even though your shoulders may be angled opened or closed toward the foul line, remember this very important point: always walk straight toward the foul line. Never drift to the right or left or walk at an angle relative to the lane.

If your shoulders are opened or closed, walk slightly on the sides of your feet so that you end up with your feet on the same boards they were on when you assumed your stance.

▶ **#10 Pin Shot**

Drifting to the right is a common problem with the #10 pin shot. The problem occurs because your angle relative to the lane is sharp, and it is difficult to walk straight to the foul line.

If you have a problem making the #10 pin, check your feet in the stance and then again after you release at the foul line. You should be no more than one or two boards from your stance position. If you find that you have drifted more than one or two boards, concentrate on reducing

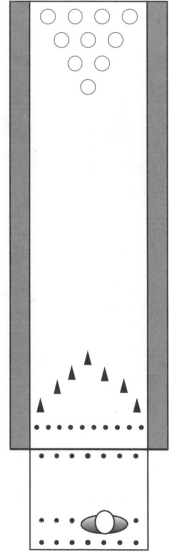

Straight shoulders

FIGURE 6-12 Shoulder alignment for head pin shots.

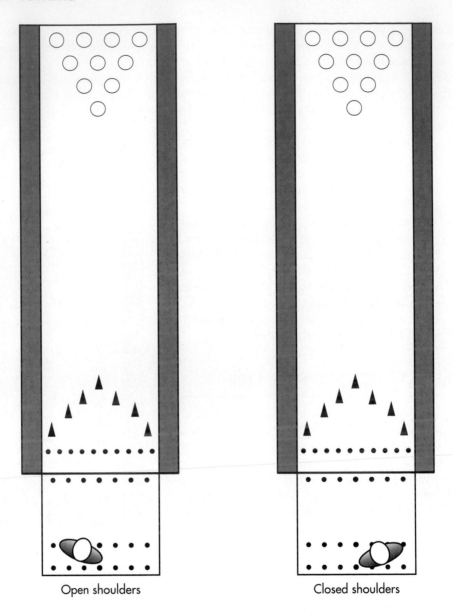

Open shoulders   Closed shoulders

FIGURE 6-13 Shoulder alignment for pins to right of head pin.

FIGURE 6-14 Shoulder alignment for pins to left of head pin.

your drift on your next #10 pin shot. Figure 6-15 shows the path of your approach on this shot with opened or closed shoulders.

Figure 6-16 is a spare conversion chart for right-handed bowlers that summarizes many of the points covered in the previous paragraphs. It may be helpful for you to refer to it the next few times you bowl.

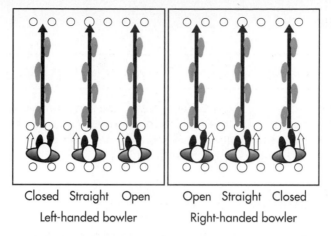

Closed	Straight	Open		Open	Straight	Closed

Left-handed bowler

Right-handed bowler

FIGURE 6-15 Avoid drift on the #10 pin shot. Always walk straight in relation to the lane.

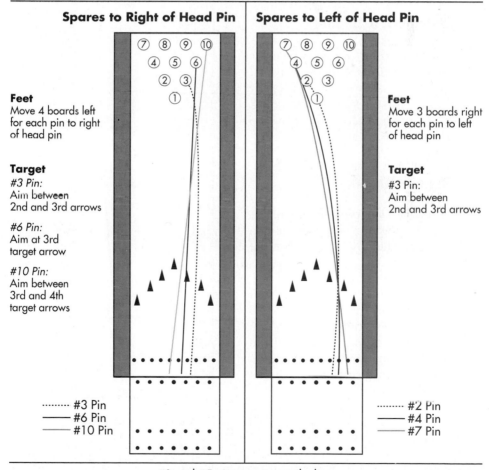

#1 and #5 pins same as strike line

FIGURE 6-16 Right-handed spare conversion chart. Make all spare adjustments based on your adjusted strike position.

MAKING SPARES: LEFT-HANDED BOWLERS

The right-handed theory for making spares is the same for left-handers except that the rules are reversed. It's like looking in a mirror. Things on your right appear to the left in the mirror's image. Other than that, everything else is the same. The same steps for right-handers apply to left-handers.

STEP 1: DETERMINE KEY PIN POSITION

Make every shot a one-pin shot, and remember that any spare can be made by aiming for the proper key pin position. Let's look at some examples.

▶ **Example 1: 6-10 Shot**

For left-handers a common spare is the 6-10. To convert this spare, your ball should strike the #6 pin, which causes it to "domino" into the #10 pin and knock it down. Figure 6-17 shows how to convert the 6-10.

▶ **Example 2: Make-Believe Shot for Left-Handers**

Sometimes no key pins are left standing. When this occurs, you need to do a make-believe shot by aiming for the place where the key position pin was standing.

Let's assume that your first shot knocked down all the pins but the #5 pin. What key position would you aim for? The #1 pin. Actually, you would aim the same as you would for a strike. Figure 6-18 shows the make-believe shot for this situation.

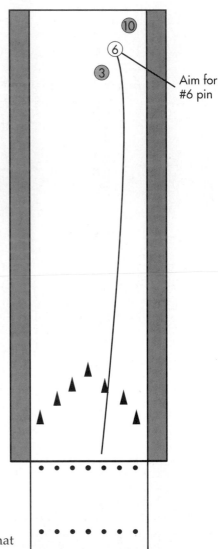

Aim for #6 pin

FIGURE 6-17 The 6-10 shot: aim for the pin that is closest to you.

▶ **Example 3: 2-7 Split**

Another common left-handed situation is the 2-7 split, another example of a baby split. In this example, do not aim for either the #2 pin or the #7 pin. If you did this, the one you didn't aim for would remain standing. Instead, aim *between* them, or where the #4 pin would be if it were standing. Figure 6-19 shows how to convert the 2-7 split.

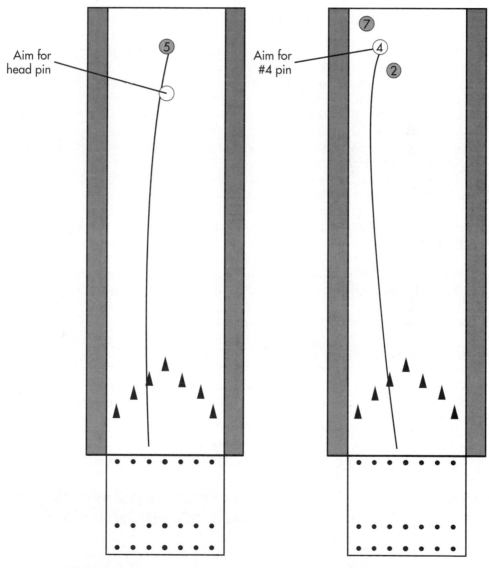

FIGURE 6-18 Make-believe shot for left-handed bowlers.

FIGURE 6-19 Converting the 2-7 split.

STEP 2: ALIGN YOUR FEET

Move either left or right of where you line up for a strike shot. For shots *to the left of the head pin, move right;* for shots *to the right of the head pin, move left.*

The tip in the accompanying box is a good rule of thumb to follow when attempting #1 and #5 pin spares.

▶ Shots to Left of Head Pin

For shots to the left of the head pin, move your stance position right four boards at a time; for example:

- For #2 pin spares, move right four boards from where you line up for a strike.
- For #4 pin spares, move right eight boards.
- For #7 pin spares, move right 12 boards.

▶ Shots to Right of Head Pin

For shots to the right of the head pin, move your stance position *left, three boards at a time;* for example:

- For #3 pin spares, move left three boards from where you line up for a strike.
- For #6 pin spares, move left six boards.
- For #10 pin spares, move left nine boards.

Figure 6-20 illustrates lining up for both situations.

By now you must be asking the question, "Why four boards for shots to the left and three boards for shots to the right?" Here's why. You are throwing against the rotation of the ball when you make spares to the left and with the rotation of the ball when you make spares to the right. The one-board difference counteracts the ball's rotational effect.

STEP 3: ALIGN YOUR TARGET

In our discussion of making strikes, we mentioned that you should aim for the second arrow when making a strike shot. This changes when you make spares. As

Performance Tip

Positioning: #1 and #5 Pin Spares

When making the #1 or the #5 pin spares, don't move right or left. Stay in your strike position.

you shift over in the stance to make a spare, the target arrow you aim for also changes. Sometimes you will aim between the target arrows. Here are some pointers you can use to align your target:

- For #1, #2, and #5 pin spares, don't change your target; use the second target arrow as you would for a strike shot.
- For all spares to the right of the head pin, aim between the second and third target arrows.
- For #4 and #7 pin spares, aim at the third target arrow.

SHOULDER ALIGNMENT WHEN MAKING SPARES

As your position in the stance and your target change, so does the angle of your body relative to the lane. Remember how we discussed how your shoulders could be opened, closed, or straight relative to the lane? We also said that for strike shots, your shoulders should be straight relative to the lane.

When making spares, this not always true. What is true is that you should *always point your body in the direction of the target.* We call this *presetting the angle of the shoulders.* Remember these three rules:

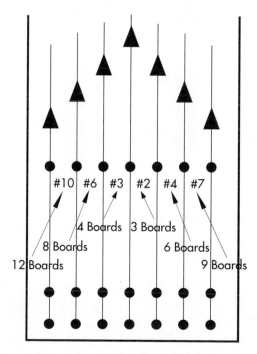

FIGURE 6-20 Lining up left or right for right-handed bowlers. (For left-handed bowlers, reverse the number of boards.)

1. When making #1 and #5 key pin position spares, keep your shoulders straight relative to the lane, just like you would when making a strike. Figure 6-21 shows how your shoulders should be aligned for these shots.
2. When making shots to the left of the head pin, open your shoulders relative to the lane. Figure 6-22 shows proper shoulder alignment for these shots.

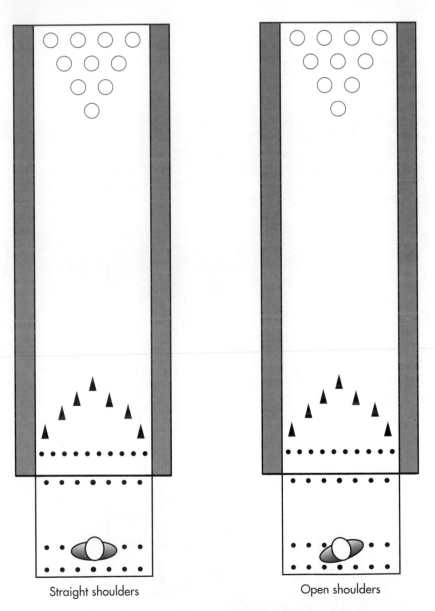

Straight shoulders

Open shoulders

FIGURE 6-21 Shoulder alignment for head pin shots.

FIGURE 6-22 Shoulder alignment for pins to left of head pin.

3. When making shots to the right of the head pin, close your shoulders relative to the lane. Figure 6-23 shows how your shoulders should be aligned for these shots.

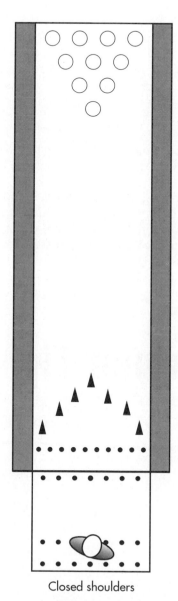

Closed shoulders

FIGURE 6-23 Shoulder alignment for pins to right of head pin.

Doing this is easy if you remember to imagine that 3-foot arrow poised on your left shoulder. Simply point the arrow at the target and your target angle will be automatically correct. The tip in the accompanying box contains some good advice for new bowlers.

WALK STRAIGHT TO FOUL LINE

Even though your shoulders may be angled opened or closed relative to the lane, remember this very important point: always walk straight to the foul line. Never drift left or right or walk at an angle relative to the lane. If your shoulders are opened or closed, walk slightly on the sides of your feet so that you end up with your feet on the same boards they were on when you assumed your stance.

▶ #7 Pin Shot

Drifting to the right is a common problem with the #7 pin shot. The problem occurs because your angle relative to the lane is sharp, and it is difficult to walk straight to the foul line.

If you have a problem making the #7 pin, check your feet in the stance and then again after you release at the foul line. You should be no more than one or two boards from your stance position. If you find that you have drifted more than one or two boards, concentrate on reducing your drift on your next #7 pin shot. Figure 6-24 shows the path of your approach on this shot with opened or closed shoulders.

The spare chart for left-handed bowlers in Figure 6-25 summarizes many of the points we covered in the previous paragraphs. It may be helpful for you to refer to it the next few times you bowl.

Performance Tip

Keep Your Armswing Consistent

Some new bowlers change their armswing out or in when aiming at an angle to the lane. *Never change your armswing.* Instead, change the angle of your shoulders.

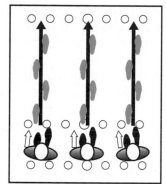

Closed   Straight   Open

FIGURE 6-24 Avoid drift on the #7 pin shot.

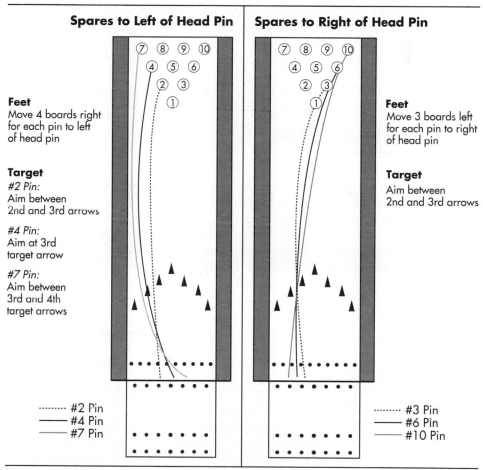

Spares to Left of Head Pin

Feet
Move 4 boards right
for each pin to left
of head pin

Target
#2 Pin:
Aim between
2nd and 3rd arrows

#4 Pin:
Aim at 3rd
target arrow

#7 Pin:
Aim between
3rd and 4th
target arrows

········· #2 Pin
———— #4 Pin
———— #7 Pin

Spares to Right of Head Pin

Feet
Move 3 boards left
for each pin to right
of head pin

Target
Aim between
2nd and 3rd arrows

········· #3 Pin
———— #6 Pin
———— #10 Pin

#1 and #5 pins same as strike line

FIGURE 6-25 Left-handed spare conversion chart. Make all spare adjustments based on your adjusted strike position.

ADJUSTING TO VARYING LANE CONDITIONS

All lanes appear very shiny. At times a bowling ball returns with an oily ring around it. This is because lane conditioner is regularly applied to the lane's surface. The conditioner helps protect the lane's wood surface and allows the ball to initially skid on the lane before it starts rolling and hooking into the pins.

As soon as oil conditioner is applied to a lane, it begins to evaporate at a rate proportional to how much the lane is being used. Overhead lighting, the porosity of the wood, and the type of conditioner also contribute to the evaporation rate.

Lane condition is important because the amount of oil on a lane determines how your ball reacts during a shot. If you have ever bowled, you may have noticed that even though you were doing everything right, you consistently missed your strike and spare shots. This was probably because there was more or less oil conditioner on the lane than the last time you bowled.

The amount of oil is not the only consideration. Where the oil is located on the lane is also important, and the overall condition of the lane is just as important. If it has been some time since the lanes were refinished, areas have probably become old and worn. All these factors affect what your ball does once it leaves your fingers. You need to be able to "read" a lane and predict how your ball will perform.

CONSISTENCY COMES FIRST

To read a lane and adjust accordingly, you must first be able to determine if your physical game and timing are proper. The way to do this is to develop a consistent game. Adjusting to lane conditions is possible only if the following are all true:

- You have an accurate, consistent armswing.
- Your armswing is timed properly with your feet movements.
- You have developed a consistent release.
- You walk straight to the foul line without drifting more than one or two boards to the right or left.

Once you have developed consistency in your physical game, you can start considering the condition of the lane and how you can adjust. For the following discussion, let's assume that you have a consistent game.

LANE CONDITIONS

The three basic lane conditions are oily, medium, and dry.

Think of these conditions as colors spread out on the lane. Dry is red, medium is white, and oily is blue. Every time you get up to bowl, try to determine which of these conditions exists. Look at the lane and ask yourself these questions:

- Can I detect any patches of oil on the lane?
- Are there any dry or worn patches where the conditioner has evaporated?
- Is there a telltale oily ring around my bowling ball, or is it fairly dry? (Ask this question after you have taken a shot on the lane and it has been returned.)

▶ How Lane Conditions Affect Your Game

If the lanes are dry, your ball will "dig in" more when it hooks. In other words, more of the sideways spin of the ball is translated into hooking power, as shown in Figure 6-26.

If you are right-handed, your ball will probably hook too far to the left. The opposite is true for left-handed bowlers; the ball will probably hook too far to the right.

Now let's examine the oily lane condition. When the lane is oily, your ball skids and slides more and little, if any, hook will result. This is because the oily lane prohibits the ball from getting enough traction to translate its spin into a hook. Figure 6-27 shows how a ball performs on an oily lane.

If you are right-handed, your ball will probably miss to the right. The opposite is true for left-handers; the ball will probably miss to the left.

If there is a medium amount of oil on the lane, no adjustments should be necessary. Just play your regular game. Figure 6-28 shows how a ball performs on a medium conditioned lane.

▶ Adjusting to Lane Conditions

We refer to adjusting to lane conditions as getting **dialed in.** In competition the game often is won by the bowler who recognizes what's happening on the lane and is the first one to get "dialed in."

The two basic guidelines for dialing into lane conditions are as follows:

1. Move in the direction of the error.
2. Go with the flow.

▶ **Dialed In**

Term used to describe the process of adjusting to lane conditions to make more strikes and spares.

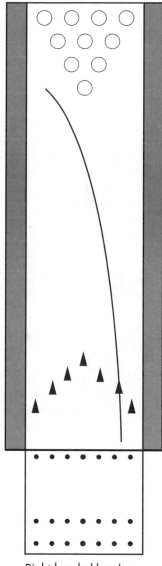

Right-handed bowler =
miss to left

Left-handed bowler =
miss to right

FIGURE 6-26 Dry lane =
more hook.

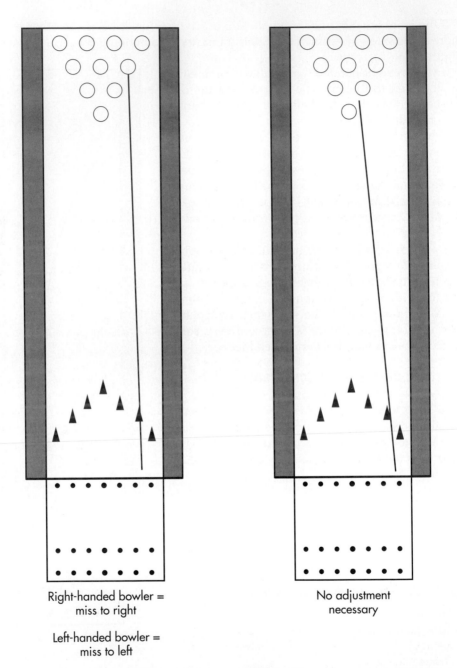

Right-handed bowler =
miss to right

Left-handed bowler =
miss to left

FIGURE 6-27 Oily lane = less hook.

FIGURE 6-28 Medium lane = medium hook.

No adjustment
necessary

MOVE IN THE DIRECTION OF THE ERROR

If your ball consistently misses to the right, move to the right in the stance. If your ball misses to the left, move to the left.

How far should you move? That depends on how far your shots are off. If you are missing four boards to the left, move over four boards, and then make fine adjustments from there to get precisely dialed in.

Aim for the same target out on the lane. Just move to the left or right in the stance. This means that you will be opening or closing your shoulders relative to the lane.

- For right-handed bowlers, open your shoulders when you adjust to the left, and close your shoulders when you adjust to the right.
- For left-handed bowlers, close your shoulders when you adjust to the left, and open your shoulders when you adjust to the right.

Figure 6-29 summarizes the adjustment process for right-handed bowlers. Figure 6-30 summarizes the adjustment process for left-handed bowlers.

Remember that even though you are adjusting to the left or right, *always walk straight to the foul line*. Check your feet position in the stance and then again at the foul line to determine if you have drifted right or left. You may want to walk slightly on the sides of your feet if you find that you are drifting.

Go With the Flow.   Going with the flow means to take full advantage of whatever lane condition is present. Here are some of the ways you can go with the flow:

- Roll a straighter ball when the lanes are oily.
- Roll a hook ball when the lanes are dry.

How can you change your ball? Remember the suitcase release and the straight ball release? Just use these release techniques relative to the lane condition.

If you try to throw a hook on an oily lane, the sideways spin on the ball makes it skid more and you lose the turn on the ball. You can produce more roll on the ball by slowing down and laying the ball down earlier (before the foul line). You can produce less hook by throwing harder or by using a straighter release.

SUMMARY

- You cannot consistently make strikes and spares unless you are familiar with the components of a lane.
- All lanes are created equal: every lane in the world is the same length and width.
- You have a better chance of making a strike if you always use a hook ball to create maximum pin action on your first shot.
- Hook has a profound effect on making strikes.
- Your strategy changes when making spares because of the pin combinations confronting your second shot.
- Math bowling involves calculating the number of boards you shift from your first shot stance to make a spare on your second shot.
- A straight ball is an effective spare maker.

- Lane conditions affect your ball's performance, and you must be able to read and adjust to varying lane conditions.

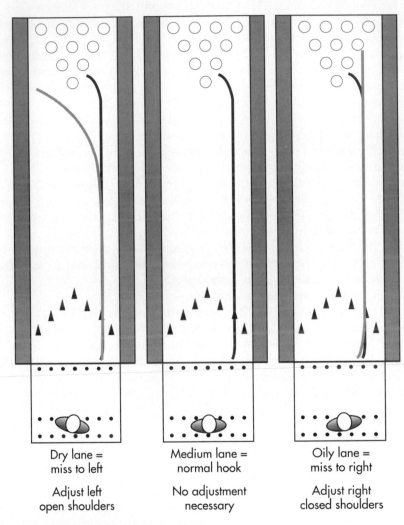

Dry lane =
miss to left

Adjust left
open shoulders

Medium lane =
normal hook

No adjustment
necessary

Oily lane =
miss to right

Adjust right
closed shoulders

FIGURE 6-29 Adjusting to a lane for right-handed bowlers. Always walk straight to the foul line—no drifting.

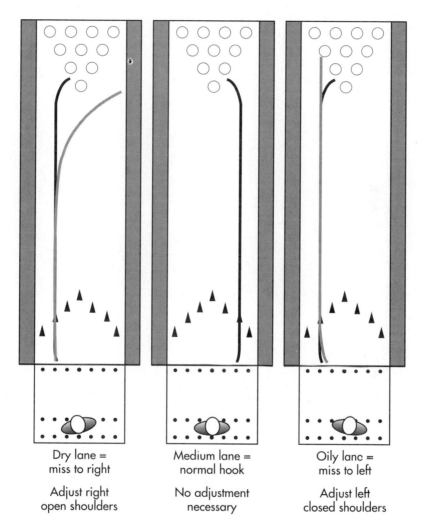

Dry lane = miss to right	Medium lane = normal hook	Oily lane = miss to left
Adjust right open shoulders	No adjustment necessary	Adjust left closed shoulders

FIGURE 6-30 Adjusting to a lane for left-handed bowlers. Always walk straight to the foul line—no drifting.

Assessment 6-1

Bowling Center Practice Drill for Spare Conversions

Name   Section   Date

The following assessment drills and checklists are designed to help you make strikes and spares. The practice drill for spare conversions should be done at a bowling center. Two spare conversion checklists are provided, one for right-handed bowlers and one for left-handed bowlers.

This practice drill combines concentrated practice on leaving a spare with the intrigue of going for the unknown.

1. Dedicate one practice day each week, and concentrate solely on making spares.
2. Bowl two shots per frame. On your first shot, aim for a spare that you have been experiencing frequently and want to work on.
3. If you don't make the spare, aim for the remaining pins on your next frame.
4. Continue with this spare until you have mastered it; then go on to another spare conversion with which you are having difficulty.

Assessment 6-2

Checklists for Taking Aim

Name _____   Section _____   Date _____

These checklists for taking aim will help you evaluate your ability to make strikes and spares. To be effective, you should memorize the techniques of the checklist.

Two taking-aim checklists are provided: one for right-handers and one for left-handers.

RIGHT-HANDED BOWLER'S TAKING-AIM CHECKLIST

1. Find your strike position
   _____ Line up with inside of left foot on twentieth board
   _____ Face lane squarely
   _____ Walk straight down the lane
   _____ Check for board drift; position at foul line should be twentieth board (+/-one board)
   _____ Repeat at least five times until limber
2. Analyze
   _____ Determine if bowling ball is hitting to the right or left of the strike pocket
   NOTE: If your delivery remains consistent:
   Dry lane = more hook
   Oily lane = less hook
   Medium lane = medium hook
3. Adjust (dial in)
   _____ Move to right if ball is hitting off to the right
   _____ Move to left if ball is hitting off to the left
   _____ Always aim for second arrow when bowling for a strike
   _____ When moving to the right, turn shoulders and body in (closed shoulders)
   _____ When moving to the left, turn shoulders and body out (opened shoulders)
   _____ When remaining in the initial position on twentieth board, square shoulders relative to the lane
   _____ No matter how body is turned, always walk straight relative to the lane
   _____ If necessary, walk slightly on the sides of your feet
4. Reading pins
   _____ Soft pocket hits (common soft pocket hits are #10, #5, and #8-#10)
      _____ If bowling ball hits or is deflected, you are too far to the right
      _____ Adjust by moving one board to the right in stance

_____ Hard pocket hits (common hard pocket hits are #4, #7, and #4-#9)
    _____ If bowling ball hits or is deflected, you are too far to the left
    _____ Adjust by moving one board to the left in stance
5. Making spares (See spare conversion chart in Figure 6-16.)
_____ Seven key pin positions for spares correspond to the seven key pins on outside of pin triangle
_____ Do not change armswing to make spares; instead, adjust stance position:
    _____ Move right for spares to the left
    _____ Move left for spares to the right
_____ Make all adjustments from dialed in strike position
_____ Move four boards to the left for each key pin position right of the #1 pin
_____ Move three boards to the right for each key pin position left of the #1 pin.

LEFT-HANDED BOWLER'S TAKING-AIM CHECKLIST

1. Find your strike position
   - _____ Line up with inside of right foot on twentieth board
   - _____ Face lane squarely
   - _____ Walk straight down the lane
   - _____ Check for board drift; position at foul line should be twentieth board (+/- 1 board)
   - _____ Repeat at least five times until limber
2. Analyze
   - _____ Determine if bowling ball is hitting to the right or left of the strike pocket
   - NOTE: If your delivery remains consistent:
   - Dry lane = more hook
   - Oily lane = less hook
   - Medium lane = medium hook
3. Adjust (dial in)
   - _____ Move to right if ball is hitting off to the right
   - _____ Move to left if ball is hitting off to the left
   - _____ Always aim for second arrow when bowling for a strike
   - _____ When moving to the left, turn shoulders and body in (closed shoulders)
   - _____ When moving to the right, turn shoulders and body out (opened shoulders)
   - _____ When remaining in the initial position on twentieth board, square shoulders relative to the lane
   - _____ No matter how body is turned, always walk straight relative to the lane
   - _____ If necessary, walk slightly on the sides of your feet
4. Reading pins
   - _____ Soft pocket hits (common soft pocket hits are #7, #5, and #7-#9)
     - _____ If bowling ball hits or is deflected, you are too far to the left
     - _____ Adjust by moving one board to the left in stance
   - _____ Hard pocket hits (common hard pocket hits are #6, #10, and #6-#10)
     - _____ If bowling ball hits or is deflected, you are too far to the right
     - _____ Adjust by moving one board to right in stance
5. Making spares (See the spare conversion chart in Figure 6-25.)
   - _____ Seven key pin positions for spares correspond to the seven key pins on outside of pin triangle
   - _____ Do not change armswing to make spares; instead, adjust stance position:
     - _____ Move right for spares to the left
     - _____ Move left for spares to the right
   - _____ Make all adjustments from dialed in strike position
   - _____ Move three boards to the left for each key pin position right of the #1 pin
   - _____ Move four boards to the right for each key pin position left of the #1 pin

KEEPING **SCORE:**
ADMINISTRATIVE DETAILS

OBJECTIVES

After reading this chapter, you should be able to do the following:

- List and define the traditional terms used when scoring a game of bowling.
- Explain the fundamentals of scorekeeping.
- Demonstrate the ability to score a game.

KEY TERMS

While reading this chapter, you will become familiar with the following terms:

- ▶ Miss
- ▶ Open Frame

- ▶ Spare
- ▶ Strike

TRADITIONAL TERMS USED IN BOWLING

As in any sports-related game, bowling has its traditional terms. A good way to describe traditional terms is to compare bowling with golf or baseball. When a golfer takes one club stroke and puts the golf ball in the cup, the scorecard shows one stroke for that hole, but it is more commonly referred to as a hole in one or an ace. In baseball, when a batter hits the ball out of the ballpark, the scoreboard reflects one run, but traditionally the batter made a home run.

Now let's look at traditional terms in bowling. Bowlers who score three strikes in a row could accumulate a score of 90 pins, but traditionally they have made a turkey. You should be familiar with some of the more common traditional terms used in bowling, such as those in accompanying box.

Traditional Bowling Terms

Term	Definition
Turkey or triple	Act of making three successive strikes
Double	Act of making two successive strikes
Open	Situation describing a frame in which not all pins are knocked down
Miss	Another name or term used for an open frame
Gutter ball	Path a ball follows right or left into a channel before it reaches the pin triangle
Perfect game, or 300 game	Perfect score of 300 is attained

FUNDAMENTALS OF SCOREKEEPING

In bowling a game consists of 10 frames. During a frame, you get two chances to knock down all the pins. If you knock down all the pins the first time, you have scored a **strike** and don't get your second shot. Instead, you go on to the next frame.

When you bowl a frame, three things can happen:
1. Strike: you knock down all the pins on your first shot.
2. **Spare:** you knock down all the pins in two shots.
3. **Open frame:** pins are standing after you have taken two shots.

Earlier in this text, you were introduced to the term split. With a split, after the first shot there are pins standing in such a way that it is difficult for you to knock them down in your second shot. In other words, you either aim between the remaining pins or skid one pin into the other(s) to knock them all down. A good example of a split is the 7-10 split, where the #7 and #10 pins remain standing. Another example of a split is a baby split. A baby split is made when you can fit the ball between the two pins that are left standing. Examples of baby splits are the 3-10 and the 3-5.

Whether a shot produces a split has nothing to do with the score. If you knock down the remaining pins, you have scored a spare; if you don't, you have an open frame.

Scoring in bowling gives you extra rewards or bonuses if you score strikes. If you score a strike, you get an opportunity to make more bonus points than if you scored a spare. Here's how it works:

- A strike is worth 10 bonus points (or pins) plus your next two shots.
- A spare is worth 10 bonus points (or pins) plus your next shot.
- An open frame is worth the number of pins you knocked down in the frame. You receive no bonus points for an open frame.

SCORECARD

Figure 7-1 shows a sample scorecard. Note that this scorecard has four lines, one for each bowler. Note also that there are 10 large squares on every line. These squares represent the 10 frames you bowl in a game.

In the right-hand corner of each of the first nine frames, note that there is a smaller square; but in the tenth frame there are three smaller squares. This is because the tenth, or last, frame of a game differs slightly from the first nine. For now, let's concentrate on the first nine frames. Figure 7-2 shows a sample frame on the scorecard.

▶ **Strike**
Term for knocking down all the pins on your first shot.

▶ **Spare**
Term for knocking down all the pins in two shots.

▶ **Open Frame**
Situation in which pins are left standing after two shots.

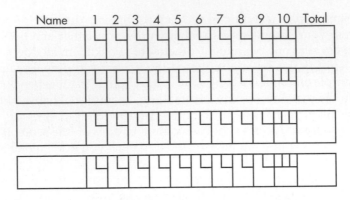

FIGURE 7-1 Sample scorecard.

The space to the left of the small square is where you record the pins you knocked down on your first shot unless you scored a strike. The small square is where you record the pins you knocked down on your second shot unless you scored a spare. The bottom half of the square is where you record your running total.

Briefly, here is how to score a frame:

1. In the space to the left of the smaller square, record the number of pins you knocked down on your first shot.
2. If you bowl an open frame, record the pins you knocked down in the smaller square.
3. If you score a strike, write an X in the smaller square.
4. If you score a spare, write a slash (/) in the smaller square.

For example, if you knocked down six pins on your first shot and two more pins on your second shot, the numbers you would record in the frame would be like Figure 7-3.

Four basic symbols are used on a scorecard.

If you make a strike, put an X in the small square. There is no need to write the number 10 to the left of the square because the X means a strike. Figure 7-4 shows how a strike is scored.

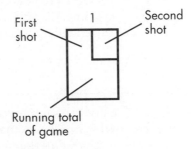

FIGURE 7-2 Sample frame.

FIGURE 7-3 Sample frame score.

FIGURE 7-4 Scoring a strike.

Note that no score was put in the running total area of the frame, because a strike is worth 10 pins plus your next two shots. You can't record the running total until you have made two more shots.

If you scored a spare, put a slash (/) in the small square. Also record the pins you knocked down on your first shot to the left of the small square. There's no need to record the score of your second shot since the slash indicates that you knocked down the remaining pins. Figure 7-5 shows how a spare is scored. In this example, the first shot knocked down nine pins.

FIGURE 7-5 Scoring a spare.

As with the example of a strike, do not fill in the running total because this spare is worth 10 points plus your next shot. You can't fill in the running total until you have made one more shot.

If you don't knock down any pins on your first shot, you have scored zero. Zero shots are identified by a dash (–) in the area to the left of the small square. If you miss all the pins on your second shot, put the dash inside the small square. Figure 7-6 shows two examples of how to score missed pins **(miss).** In the first example, the first shot missed all the pins, and the second knocked down six pins for a running total of six pins. In the second example, the first shot knocked down six pins, and the second missed the remaining pins for a running total of six pins.

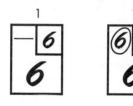

FIGURE 7-6 Scoring missed pins.

Sometimes a bowler will circle the number to the left of the small square. This indicates that the bowler was left with a split for the second shot. Using the circle has no effect on the bowler's score; it just signifies a difficult second shot.

TENTH FRAME

Figure 7-7 shows the tenth frame of a scorecard. The tenth frame is scored a bit differently from the previous frames. In the tenth frame it is possible to get up to three shots. That is why there are three small squares in this frame.

The reason that the tenth frame is different is because you have to be able to finish out the game. Suppose you make a strike on the first shot in the tenth frame. According to what you have learned so far, a strike is worth

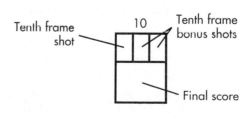

FIGURE 7-7 Tenth frame of a scorecard.

▶ **Miss**

Act of not knocking down all pins during two shots or one frame.

10 points plus your next two shots. However, there are no more frames to be played; the tenth frame is the last. That is why you have the opportunity to make up to two extra shots in the tenth frame.

Here are the general rules for scoring the tenth frame:
- If you make a strike, you get two extra shots.
- If you make a spare, you get one extra shot.
- If you open or leave pins standing, you get no extra shots.

The following examples should help clarify how to score the tenth frame. In these examples you are the bowler.

▶ Example 1

You begin the tenth frame with a running total of 150 points. On your first shot you score a strike. This means you get two more shots to finish the game. On your next shot you knock down nine pins, and on your final shot you miss the remaining pin. The ninth and tenth frames of your scorecard would look like Figure 7-8.

Adding up your shots on the tenth frame is simple; just add them all up.

▶ Example 2

In this example your score in the ninth frame is 160. On your first shot you knock down nine pins. On your next shot you knock down the remaining pin for a spare, which awards you one bonus shot. In a normal frame you would be finished, but in the tenth frame, you must take this shot to finish out the game. So, on your bonus shot, you knock down nine pins. Your total score for the tenth frame is 19, which is added to 160 to give you a final score of 179. Figure 7-9 shows how this example would be scored.

In this example a pin is left standing at the end of the game. In this case, before another person can bowl, all the pins must be set. In bowling centers there is a reset button on or near the ball return that you must push to reset the pins for the next bowler.

▶ Example 3

This time you enter the tenth frame with a score of 165. On your first shot you knock down eight pins. On your next shot, you knock down one more pin for a running total of nine. Because you didn't roll a strike or a spare, you get no bonus shots, and the nine pins you knocked down are added to your ninth frame score to produce a final score of 174. Figure 7-10 shows how this example is scored.

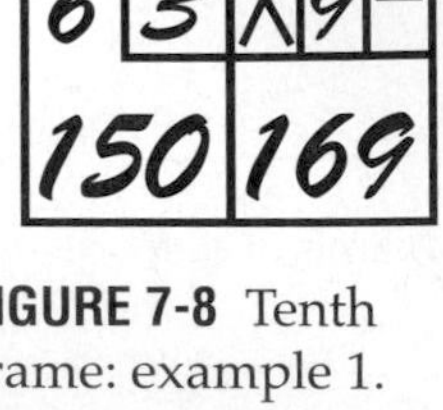

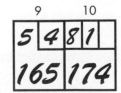

FIGURE 7-8 Tenth frame: example 1.

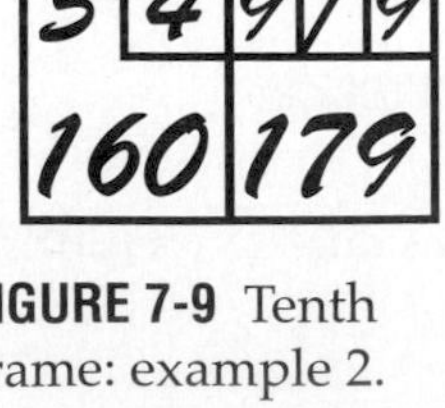

FIGURE 7-9 Tenth frame: example 2.

FIGURE 7-10 Tenth frame: example 3.

SCORING A SAMPLE GAME

The following hypothetical game demonstrates everything you have learned in this chapter. If you can follow the steps frame by frame, you will have no difficulty scoring your own game.

FIRST FRAME

Your first shot knocks down six pins, and you score a spare on the second. Figure 7-11 shows how you score the first frame. Leave the first frame's running total blank for now because your spare is worth 10 points plus your next shot.

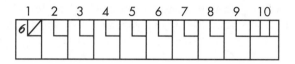

FIGURE 7-11 Scoring the first frame.

SECOND FRAME

Your first shot is a strike. Because of the spare you made in the first frame, you add the value of your strike (10 points) to the 10 points you scored in the first frame (10 + 10 = 20). Record this value in the running total area of the first frame as shown in Figure 7-12. Leave the second frame's running total blank because your strike is worth 10 points plus your next two shots.

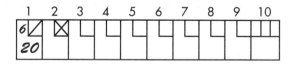

FIGURE 7-12 Scoring the second frame.

THIRD FRAME

Your first shot knocks down eight pins, and you miss the remaining pins on your next shot. Now fill in the second frame's running total:

$$20 + 10 + 8 = 38$$

Then fill in the third frame's running total:

$$38 + 8 = 46$$

Figure 7-13 shows how to score this frame.

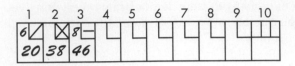

FIGURE 7-13 Scoring the third frame.

FOURTH AND FIFTH FRAMES

Since you are beginning to warm up, you bowl strikes in the fourth and fifth frames. Figure 7-14 shows how to score these frames. Place an X in the small square in both frames, but don't fill in any scores yet since a strike is worth 10 points plus your next two shots.

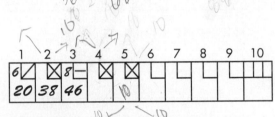

FIGURE 7-14 Scoring the fourth and fifth frames.

SIXTH FRAME

Your first shot knocks down nine pins, and you knock down the remaining pin on your second shot for a spare. Now fill in the running totals for the fourth frame:

$$46 + 10 + 10 + 9 = 75$$

Then fill in the running totals for the fifth frame:

$$75 + 10 + 9 + 1 = 95$$

Figure 7-15 shows how to score the sixth frame.

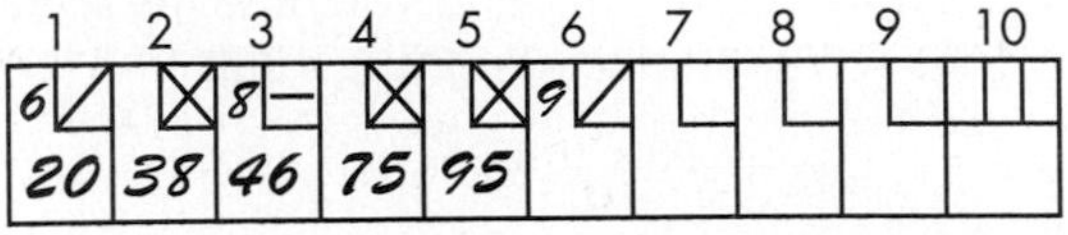

FIGURE 7-15 Scoring the sixth frame.

SEVENTH FRAME

Your first shot knocks down nine pins, and your second shot misses. Fill in the running totals for the sixth frame:

$$95 + 10 + 9 = 114$$

Then fill in the running totals for the seventh frame:

$$114 + 9 = 123$$

Figure 7-16 shows how to score the seventh frame.

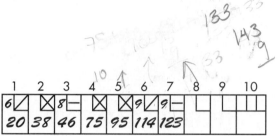

FIGURE 7-16 Scoring the seventh frame.

EIGHTH AND NINTH FRAMES

You roll strikes in these frames. Again, place an X in the small squares for these frames, but do not fill in any running totals.

TENTH FRAME

Your first shot knocks down nine pins. Now fill in the running totals for the eighth frame:

$$123 + 10 + 10 + 9 = 152$$

You score a spare on your second shot. Now fill in the running totals for the ninth frame:

$$152 + 10 + 9 + 1 = 172$$

Because it is the tenth frame and you made a spare, you take your bonus shot and make a strike. Total the three shots you made in the tenth frame, and add them to your running total to calculate your final score:

$$172 + 9 + 1 + 10 = 192$$

Figure 7-17 shows how to score the eighth, ninth, and tenth frames.

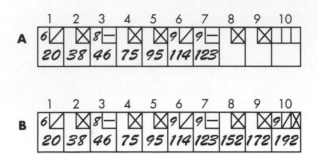

FIGURE 7-17 Scoring the eighth and ninth **(A)** and tenth **(B)** frames.

PERFECT GAME: 300

The highest score you can attain in bowling is 300, a perfect score. To achieve 300, you must roll 12 consecutive strikes. Figure 7-18 shows a scorecard for a 300 game.

Can you see how a perfect game is scored? Remember the scoring rules and try scoring this game frame by frame.

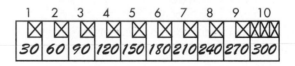

FIGURE 7-18 A perfect game.

SUMMARY

- Bowling, like most other sports, has unique and traditional terms with which you should be familiar.
- A defined method for keeping score has been established for use throughout the world.

CHAPTER 8

THE **MENTAL GAME:**
HOW TO MASTER IT

OBJECTIVES

After reading this chapter, you should be able to do the following:

- Promote positive self-talk and affirmations.
- Prepare yourself to perform when it is your turn to bowl.
- Establish a positive approach to your approach.
- Practice positive visualization and mental imagery.
- Create relaxing atmospheres both outside and inside a bowling center.
- Establish process-oriented goals.
- Explain how exercise and nutrition enhance your mental and physical game.

KEY TERMS

While reading this chapter, you will become familiar with the following terms:

- ► Affirmations
- ► Goal Ladder
- ► Mental Skills
- ► Self-Talk

BOWLING: THE MENTAL GAME

There are few sports where the psychology of the athlete comes more into play than bowling. Although bowling can be a team sport, when it comes time to bowl it's totally one-on-one. There's you, and there's your opponent: the lane pins.

Keep in mind that the biggest secret to a good mental game is to possess the skill to succeed and feel confident in this skill. Confidence is the basis of a winning attitude. Remember:

Competence = Confidence

POSITIVE SELF-TALK

All of us have a silent inner voice that either encourages or discourages us. Encouraging statements can be a promising statement of some future accomplishment or an acknowledgment of a job well done. Discouraging statements include worrying about the future or criticizing yourself for making a mistake. **Affirmations** are positive self-talk statements. A common one used at Team USA is ICE, an acronym for "I Carry Everything" or "I Can Strike on Every Shot."

Team USA is composed of six women and six men who qualified for the team by demonstrating their bowling skills at competitions held at a local level. They then advanced to a national competition where they were selected to the team by process of elimination after bowling 24 qualifying games followed by 24 head-to-head match play games. These six men and six women were the top 12 after the 48 games were completed. For 1 year they represent the United States in national and international bowling competition. Team USA trains at the Olympic Training Center and competes in 10 to 20 bowling matches held in the United States and throughout the world. Team USA bowlers undergo a great deal of stress when qualifying and playing for the team, and they have developed a number of strategies to perform well under stress.

When Team USA bowlers line up to make strikes, they take a deep breath, hold it, and think "ICE." Concentrating on this positive statement just before bowling improves performance.

We call the comments your inner voice makes **self-talk.** Encouraging statements are *positive self-talk*. Discouraging statements are *negative self-talk*.

Positive self-talk is more than glib statements about past or current accomplishments. Consider the following statements:

- Negative: "I don't think I'll ever get that #10 pin spare down right."
- Positive: "Next week, I'm going to practice on just #10 pin shots until I have the angle and target dialed in."

▶ **Affirmations**
  Positive self-talk statements.

▶ **Self-Talk**
  Mental thoughts a person conceives and transmits through inner voices. Self-talk thoughts can be both negative and positive.

Both statements reflect a current inability to perform a desired goal. The first statement, however, is a statement of frustration and defeat. The second statement looks positively toward the future, constructing a game plan for eventual success.

SELF-TALK AT HOME

What works in the bowling center works at home too. Developing and maintaining a positive mental attitude are a full-time endeavor. Often, before bowlers retire for the evening on the day before a big match, they will spend a few minutes getting psyched up for the game and silently (or verbally) recite their affirmations. These can be personal affirmations (which we strongly encourage you adopt) or stock affirmations, such as the ones we will provide.

Often, developing a self-talk tape filled with affirmations, imagery of bowling well, and relaxation techniques (which we'll cover later) helps. Every bowler for Team USA has such a tape, often set to music of his or her choice.

SAMPLE AFFIRMATIONS

The accompanying boxes (pp. 137-140) are organized by category. Make use of the items that are appropriate to you and incorporate them—along with your own affirmations—into a self-talk tape.

Performance Tip

Preparing for Provocation

- This is going to upset me, but I know how to deal with it.
- What is it that I have to do?
- I can work out a plan to handle this.
- Remember to stick to the issues and not take it personally.
- I can manage the situation. I know how to regulate my anger.
- If I find myself getting upset, I'll know what to do.
- There won't be any need for an argument.
- Try not to take this too seriously.
- This could be a testy situation, but I believe in myself.
- Take time for a few deep breaths of relaxation.
- Feel comfortable, relaxed, and at ease.
- Easy does it. Remember to keep your sense of humor.

PREPARING TO PERFORM
WHEN IT'S YOUR TURN TO BOWL

Before you get up to bowl or as you line up in your stance, establish a positive mental attitude by concentrating on the following:

1. *Focus on what you are about to do.* Visualize a big sign hanging from the ceiling that reads, "Focus."
2. *Relax by breathing.* Breathe normally in through your nose and out through your mouth.
3. *Practice positive mental imagery.* See yourself executing a perfect walk, swing, finish, and release.
4. *Remember the line in your mind.* Visualize the line in your mind just before you commit to the approach.

If you have concentrated on the four points mentioned in the previous section, there's nothing left to do; you are focused and ready. Commit yourself to the approach, take your first step, and *just do it!*

Performance Tip

Coping With Confrontation

- Stay calm. Just continue to relax.
- As long as I keep my cool, I'm in control.
- Just roll with the punches. Don't get bent out of shape.
- Think of what you want to get out of this.
- You don't need to prove yourself.
- There is no point in getting mad.
- Don't make more out of this than you have to. I'm not going to let them get to me.
- Look for the positives. Don't assume the worst or jump to conclusions.
- It's really a shame that players have to act like this.
- For someone to be that irritable, he or she must be very unhappy.
- If I start to get mad, I'll just be banging my head against the wall.
- I might as well just relax. There is no need to doubt myself.
- What they say doesn't matter. I'm on top of the situation.
- Everything's under control.

Performance Tip

Coping With Sudden Stress

- My muscles are starting to feel tight. Time to relax and slow down. Grip the ball as if it were a baby kitten.
- Getting upset won't help.
- It's just not worth it to get so angry.
- I'll let them make fools of themselves.
- I have a right to be annoyed, but let's keep the lid on.
- It's time to take a deep breath.
- Let's take the issue point by point.
- My anger is a signal of what I need to do. Time to instruct myself.
- I'm not going to get pushed around, but I'm not going haywire either.
- Try to reason it out. Treat each other with respect.
- Let's try a cooperative approach. Maybe we are both right.
- Negatives lead to more negatives. Work constructively.
- They'd probably like me to get really angry. Well, I'm going to disappoint them.
- I can't expect people to act the way I want them to.
- Take it easy. Don't get pushy.

VISUALIZATION AND IMAGERY: WHAT YOU SEE IS WHAT YOU GET!

Visualization can be referred to as the pictures or thoughts that go through our minds. The human brain has a tremendous capacity to process such information. The nature of these visions can have a tremendous effect on our performances in different situations. If these visions are positive, they are more likely to enhance performance than if they are negative. I'm sure we've all visualized an error at some time or other and then proceeded to make it (or watch it) happen! If you are concerned with performance, it is probably important to learn to direct and focus the "human computer." This might take the form of "parking" (clearing the mind of negative thoughts, images, and cues) or positive visualization (focusing on performance-enhancing cues, images, and behaviors).

Performance Tip

Reflecting on Provocation

When Conflict Is Unresolved

- Forget about the aggravation. Thinking about it only makes you upset.
- These are difficult situations. They take time to straighten out.
- Try to shake it off. Don't let it interfere with your job.
- I'll get better at this as I get more practice.
- Remember relaxation. It's a lot better than anger.
- Can you laugh about it? It's probably not so serious.
- Don't take it personally.
- Take a deep breath and think positive thoughts.

When Conflict Is Resolved or Coping Is Successful

- I handled that one pretty well. It worked!
- That wasn't as hard as I thought.
- It could have been a lot worse.
- I could have gotten more upset than it was worth.
- I actually got through that without getting angry.
- When I don't take my pride too seriously, I'm better off.
- I've been getting upset for too long when it wasn't even necessary.
- I'm doing better at this all the time.

PAYOFFS

Why is visualization important? Positive visualization has numerous payoffs.

1. It prepares the body and mind for activity. With vivid positive visualization, similar neurological activity to those muscle groups used in performing a specific task take place, and this is often effective in readying the mind and body for action.
2. Visualization facilitates "parking," clearing potential distraction or negative random thoughts and visions. The mind always seems to be processing something. Even at times when we suggest our mind goes blank, it doesn't take long before one starts to process something about blankness or its significance!

Even during sleep, there is considerable indication of brain (electroencephalographic) activity. The mind is always doing something.

3. It facilitates narrowing of your focus to task-relevant cues. Visualizing "keeping your eye on the puck," "reading a defense," or "bowling a strike," for example, helps you narrow your focus to the cues you need to do the job well.

4. Visualization builds or rebuilds confidence and adaptability. As humans we are all prone to the recency effect—overweighing the last thing that happened to us or went through our mind. Through positive visualization of past or future performance possibilities, we enhance our feelings of confidence, competence, and control and counteract our tendency to overreact to a negative thought, disappointing performance, or disappointing result. Visualization can help make optimists out of pessimists!

5. It can be energizing or relaxing or both, depending on its content. Visualizing positive performance and behavior images can also often help people who have been worrying to relax, especially if the visualization is of relaxed and composed performance, behavior, and images.

6. It is an effective response to worrying. If you are going to worry (that is, think about negative possibilities), why not rehearse a positive response to some of these possibilities. Some worry is not bad if it motivates you to rehearse a response to some of the possibilities you might face. If you are going to worry, do some positive worrying and turn potential problems into opportunities to test yourself!

7. It is an effective way to practice, develop, and automate physical skills and **mental skills.** It has been suggested that "practice does not make perfect" but "perfect practice makes perfect." Quality may be more important than quantity in practicing skills!

The exciting thing about positive visualization (mental practice) is that you can be successful more often than you usually can in physical practice. Success in positive visualization is probably more important than success in physical practice in learning and automating both physical skills and mental skills.

NOTE: Mental skills are the ability to focus in a way that produces desirable results. As mentioned earlier, the neurological activity involved in positive visualization probably enhances the learning and automating of skills.

How do you do it? Are there secrets? Individuals differ in what is most effective in improving the effectiveness of their visualization. Although most of us could become much more effective in directing and harnessing the human computer, there are those who argue that most of us only realize 10% to 20% of our potential!

In striving to improve visualization, it is important to have a few factors to think about. Consider focusing primarily on the process of performance rather than the product (consequences). When asked what they do when the coach asks them to think about the game, these two responses from 10-year veteran hockey players are not all that uncommon:

▶ **Mental Skills**
The ability to focus in a way that produces desirable results.

- Player 1: "I pretend I'm Gretzky and start visualizing how I'm going to play out there. I see myself anticipating, skating, passing, scoring, assisting, and supporting my teammates."
- Player 2: "I think about how important the game might be to me, my friends, my coach, my dad and mom . . . what might happen if we win or especially if we lose. . . .

We'll leave it to you to figure out who might actually perform better in most games!

Consider focusing primarily on goals within your control (personal and situational excellence) versus things beyond your control (officials' calls, opponents' behavior). You can't directly control these things, but you can control your response to them and develop possible solutions.

WORRYING

The following quote has been attributed to Mickey Rivers (major league baseball player and philosopher): "Ain't no use worryin 'bout things beyond your control, cause if they're beyond your control, ain't no use worryin. . . ."

Certainly there is merit in focusing primarily on goals within your control. Some performance goals are considerably beyond your control (scores in games, external ratings, rankings, etc.). Top athletes such as Ingmar Stemnark, Graham Smith, and Wayne Gretzky seem to have accomplished as much as they have by focusing primarily on self-improvement, personal and situational excellence goals, and letting the consequences and outcomes take care of themselves.

ENVIRONMENT

Be aware that the environment you will be facing may include varying circumstances. Consider spending approximately 90% of your visualizing time focusing on your response to anticipated conditions.

Consider spending approximately 10% of your visualizing time focusing on your response to surprises (unusual circumstances) so you have at least rehearsed a positive coping response and will be much more likely to respond or feel positively in varying circumstances.

Also try to visualize your responses in the physical environment and conditions you expect. Obviously, if you have performed in a similar environment before, this is greatly facilitated. (Creative athletes and coaches, however, are great at physically or mentally simulating similar conditions in which to rehearse their responses!)

SEQUENCE

- Consider following through each vision situation to a successful conclusion. When mentally rehearsing, consider dealing with one situation at a time (sequentially) to avoid feelings of overload or lack of control.

- Consider repeating components if necessary or valuable for readiness, confidence, and feelings of control.
- Consider visualizing with desired speed and control. If you tend to be too tentative or conservative, consider visualizing performing with more assertiveness, quickness, and agility.
- Consider trying to visualize as vividly as possible. Sometimes attending to different sensory sources when visualizing (sight, sound, smell, taste, feel) can increase the quality and effectiveness of your visions or mental rehearsal.

BE CREATIVE

In sports and physical activity, visual and kinesthetic sensors are probably the key ones to enhance visualization and performance. Attending to the feeling of a good performance when visualizing seems to be particularly valuable.

Creative visualizers might attend to one sense at a time and then integrate them for top-quality visualization!

Consider a "past," "future," and "now" sequence in your visualization and preparation, when time permits. Recalling a past performance highlight can sometimes get you immersed in a desired response. Then you project the vision into a future possibility context and finally focus on the current opportunity.

WHEN AND WHERE?

When and where should visualization take place? Consider positive visualization whenever you have time for it and are seeking one of the payoffs outlined above. Be creative and learn to use this mental skill in a variety of circumstances or situations as suggested in the box on p. 144. Remember, when combined with physical effort and practice, positive visualization may lead to considerably better results and more satisfaction.

GUIDED VISUALIZATION/RELAXATION: EXAMPLE

Find a quiet place where you will not be disturbed for 15 minutes. Sit in a comfortable chair, or lie on the floor. Close your eyes. Bring your focus inward and center on your breathing . . . breathe in deeply . . . filling your belly and chest, and exhale fully . . . breathe in relaxation and peace . . . exhale tension and worry . . . breathe . . . begin to concentrate on your center . . . an area about 2 inches below or 2 inches above your navel . . . whichever feels most comfortable to you . . . connect with this center . . . this power . . . this strength . . . now, begin to feel the energy at the top of your head . . . experience it moving down to your shoulders . . . down your back . . . down through the base of your spine and out the bottom of your feet like roots . . . down through the floor and deep into the earth . . . strong, sturdy roots deep into the earth . . . spreading . . . connecting, making you secure and solid . . . continue to focus on your center, feeling the energy and power in that area. . . .

Performance Tip

When and Where Visualization Can Help

- As you awaken and start your day
- When situationally waiting and readying to perform (Between periods, hockey players can be visualizing their response to everything happening on the ice as if they were out there.)
- When traveling to and from games, practices, and school
- In conjunction with music
- Instead of watching TV (especially commercials)
- When reviewing, goal setting, and planning (past, future, and now)
- Before falling asleep each night
- As part of an injury rehabilitation program

Remember: "What you see is often what you get," so if you want things to happen, working on positive visualization may be a valuable first or complementary step.

When you exhale, imagine any tension in your body going deep into the earth through the roots you have established . . . when you inhale, feel the earth's energy coming up into your body through your spine and up into your heart center just behind your breast bone . . . imagine the earth's energy passing through your heart's center and out into the world around you . . . see and feel any uneven, unfocused energy you might have in your body flowing down into the earth to be dispelled as you exhale . . . see and feel the bright earth's energy flowing upward into your spine and out through your heart center into your environment . . . feel the peace and connectedness in your body . . . the lightness . . . the focused awareness connecting you with people and your environment on a deep, confident, and relaxed level . . . as you feel this newfound sense of tranquility and centeredness in your body, note that your mind has calmed and you are in control of your feelings and thoughts . . . gently breathing in . . . bringing in new earth energy to your body . . . exhaling through your heart center . . . relaxation, peace and centeredness spreading throughout your body. . . .

Allow your mind to think of a place . . . a beautiful place . . . a place where you are safe and free . . . a place where you feel confident and powerful. It can be any place—real or imaginary . . . a meadow . . . a beach . . . a mountaintop . . . a hidden waterfall . . . any place that is your place . . . you feel nurtured here . . . you feel beautiful and important here. Find a comfortable spot to stand in your favorite place . . . an energy spot . . . and center yourself there, quieting your body and your mind, being at peace and one with this spot . . . follow it with your eyes . . . as you come to the end of this path, you are aware of a gentle mist flowing along the path coming towards you . . . enveloping your body in a soft blue light.

Be aware of how this delicate blue mist makes you feel as it gently moves around your belly and your chest to your heart . . . what emotions come up for you? . . . what do you feel in your body? You feel peaceful as the mist moves away from you down the path and disappears from your view. . . .

As you turn to look in a new direction, you are aware of a slow-moving green mist drifting toward you . . . you are not afraid . . . you welcome it as it envelops you in a soft, gentle, green cloud. . . .

Note its shade and become aware of how it makes you feel as it reaches your heart with its delicate color. It is a soft and healing color. Slowly . . . slowly . . . you let it go. It floats away toward the horizon and out of sight . . . you are happy and feel whole and full of peace.

You note a small pink cloud moving towards you . . . it almost looks like cotton . . . fluffy . . . pink . . . velvety . . . coming to you and filling your heart with tenderness . . . softness . . . compassion . . . lightness . . . joy . . . and love. You feel so safe and whole . . . . Connect with the feelings and sounds that come up for you and surrender to them as the cloud holds you in its pinkness for a moment . . . then quietly . . . smoothly . . . it moves through your heart and into the distance and is gone. . . .

You stand alone now, calmly . . . waiting . . . a warm glow touches your head . . . moving slowly down through your hair . . . over your ears and yellow color . . . warmth sprinkling down on you . . . flowing over your shoulders and down your body past your hips . . . down your legs, spilling all around your feet like a tissue gown . . . warm and light . . . filling you with wisdom, confidence and well-being. You stand there in the glow and the light . . . aware of your intelligence and abilities . . . thanking your body, mind, and spirit for their gifts to you . . . you have everything you need to be . . . do and have what you wish . . . . The gold forms a beautiful, feathery cloud above you, and you feel light and free of the earth beneath your feet . . . . Allow yourself to float with the golden cloud above you until you become so small and faint that the picture is gone and all is quiet. . . .

Slowly begin to return to the steady pace of your breathing . . . inhaling deeply . . . holding . . . exhaling . . . breathing . . . knowing that any time you need to relax . . . anytime you need to center yourself . . . you need only to think of the colors . . . blue . . . green . . . pink . . . gold . . . and remember your special place of power, confidence, peace, and tranquility.

Begin to reconnect with the room now. Feel the chair or floor beneath you now as you slowly bring the roots back up into the soles of your feet . . . up your legs and into your spine . . . hear the sounds around you . . . breathe.

Count to three and open your eyes, feeling refreshed and relaxed. Move your fingers and toes . . . breathing deeply . . . reconnecting with your body . . . . Move your head and shoulders . . . coming back into the energy of the room around you . . . knowing you have everything you need to be relaxed and confident . . . . Open your eyes when you are ready. . . .

SEQUENTIAL RELAXATION

Sequential relaxation uses the exhalation phase of your breathing cycle to relax specific body parts in detail.

To perform this technique, you do the following:

1. Focus your attention on a specific body part.
2. Feel the sensations of relaxation occurring in the body part that you are focusing on while you exhale and only while you exhale.
3. Move your attention to the corresponding body part if there is one (for example, from right foot and ankle to left foot and ankle) or to the next body part in sequence.
4. Move throughout your body in sequence until the entire body has been covered (foot; lower leg; upper leg; lower torso and hips; the trunk including the shoulders, arms, and hands).
5. Remain in the relaxed state until you are ready to end the exercise and then take a deep breath as you flex, stretch, and open your eyes.

GUIDED RELAXATION

The following is an example of a guided relaxation session. Use it as a guide to develop your own relaxation tape. (Some very good visualization and relaxation tapes are available in stores. Instead of making one of your own, you might try a store-bought tape.)

Assume a comfortable position, and when ready, allow your eyes to close. For several breathing cycles, quietly and passively listen to yourself breathe . . . .

And now turn your attention to just the exhalation phase of your breathing cycle . . . and r-e-l-a-x as you exhale. . . . Simply permit yourself to l-e-t g-o . . . and r-e-l-a-x more with each exhalation.

Now focus on your right foot and ankle and, as you exhale, note the tension flow out of that foot and ankle . . . note that foot and ankle become slightly heavy and more and more r-e-l-a-x-e-d. . . . As you note this, allow your foot and ankle to s-i-n-k d-o-w-n and become totally supported by the supporting environment. . . .

And now, focus your attention on the left foot and ankle . . . and allow it to let go and r-e-l-a-x with your exhalations. . . . Allow that foot and ankle to become slightly h-e-a-v-y . . . and more and more relaxed with each exhalation.

At this time, move your attention to your right lower leg (the calf region). . . . As you focus on this area, allow the muscles to r-e-l-a-x . . . to l-e-t g-o as you exhale . . . simply allow the tensions to flow out of your lower leg as you e-x-h-a-l-e . . . and r-e-l-a-x. . . .

Move your attention to your lower left leg and, with each exhalation, feel the muscles of the left lower leg s-i-n-k-i-n-g d-o-w-n . . . and becoming h-e-a-v-y . . . . And now, move your attention to your right thigh . . . and feel that part of your body r-e-l-a-x as you exhale . . . and r-e-l-a-x as you exhale. . . .

Now, focus your attention on your left thigh. Feel and experience a l-e-t-t-i-n-g g-o with each exhalation. . . .

Focus now on both legs and note a comfortable heaviness develop with each exhalation as you experience the gentle pull of gravity on your legs. . . .

And now, let the relaxation in your legs flow into the lower torso and hips . . . As you exhale, allow the muscles to r-e-l-a-x and feel the lower torso s-i-n-k-i-n-g d-o-w-n into the supporting environment as you exhale. . . .

Now, let this relaxation flow into the trunk area as you exhale and r-e-l-a-x. Feel your trunk sinking down and becoming c-o-m-f-o-r-t-a-b-l-y h-e-a-v-y . . . and more and more r-e-l-a-x-e-d with each exhalation.

Now, allow this relaxation to flow into your entire body with each exhalation. Feel, sense, and experience a comfortable heaviness . . . or a general slowing down of your body . . . Allow your body now to establish its own pace and r-e-l-a-x as you exhale. . . .

Allow this relaxation to occur throughout your body until you are ready to end the exercise. Then take a deep breath as you flex, stretch, and open your eyes.

IMPLEMENTATION

The guided and sequential relaxation exercises require about 7 or 8 minutes when performed as suggested in the text above. However, after a day or two of performing the technique, you should be able to shorten it to a 3- to 5-minute period.

GUIDE TO GOAL SETTING

In order to set goals, you must have a definite idea about your goal. The best way to form an idea is to identify your goal by writing it down. After writing down your goal, also write any pertinent thoughts about how you would go about achieving it. This is called a *process*. Assessment 8-1, at the end of this chapter, will guide you through a series of steps that provide a process you can use to set and realize a goal.

After you have written down your goal, the next step is to identify the steps you need to take to achieve your goal. One way to do this is to use a *ladder approach* to write down the steps in reverse order. Step 1 is at the bottom of the **goal ladder,** and the final step is at the top. Make sure the steps you identify are small and manageable. If they are not, divide them until they are. Assessment 8-2 gives an example you can use for your ladder approach.

▶ **Goal Ladder**
A written process by which the steps required are listed in reverse order, the first step at the bottom and the final step at the top.

NUTRITION, EXERCISE, AND THE MENTAL GAME

How you treat your body affects your mental attitude and ultimately your game. This brief section provides some general guidelines concerning proper nutrition and exercise. Many excellent books have been written on nutrition and exercise for sports. Consider bowling as any other aerobic sport and train as an athlete accordingly.

NUTRITION

From a nutritional standpoint, the use of stimulants and depressants probably has the biggest effect on your game. Stimulants, such as caffeine or sugar, can be used judiciously to adjust your arousal state. Depressants, such as alcohol, are discouraged during competition, because they adversely affect reaction time, coordination, and performance.

People have different levels of arousal or excitement. If a person is overaroused, his or her performance is inhibited because of anxiety and a tightening of the muscles of the body. The performance of a person who is underaroused is also adversely affected. Concentration diminishes, adrenalin levels are lowered, the desire to win diminishes, and the brain functions slower. The optimal arousal state varies from bowler to bowler. Some bowlers bowl better when they feel aggressive and excited. Others do better when they are fully relaxed and focused. To determine your optimal arousal state, ask yourself how you feel when you are really bowling well. This will be your optimal arousal state.

Many factors we've already discussed in this chapter, such as self-talk, visualization, and relaxation, affect your arousal state. Nutrition also plays a role.

Obviously, if you've just finished a big meal before bowling, you're going to feel less aroused. Conversely, if you haven't eaten anything that day, your arousal state will be diminished. If you are bowling the next day in a big tournament, it's a good idea to "carbo out," eating high-carbohydrate, starchy foods, such as pasta dishes. This will give you sustaining energy during the tournament. Sweets and stimulants, such as candy bars and coffee, tend to increase an individual's arousal state. These can be used judiciously to adjust your arousal state to a higher level, or they can be avoided to maintain your arousal state at a more moderate level. Prudence and moderation are the keys.

EXERCISE

Probably the most important exercises bowlers can take advantage of are loosening and stretching exercises. Stretching exercises prepare the body for athletic competition and prevent injuries.

Stretching exercises can also be combined with relaxation and breathing techniques to relieve anxiety and prepare the body mentally for competition. Consult any of a number of books on exercise and build a regimen of loosening and stretching exercises. Take 15 minutes each day and practice these loosening exercises. It's a good idea to *always practice stretching exercises immediately before bowling.*

Chapter 9 contains a comprehensive list of stretching exercises, with instructions how to perform them, for you to consider as a bowling exercise program.

SUMMARY

- You can become a better bowler if you promote positive self-talk and affirmations and practice positive visualization and mental imagery.
- You must prepare yourself to perform when it is your turn to bowl.
- You must establish a positive approach to your approach.
- You can create relaxing atmospheres outside and inside a bowling center if you practice positive self-talk, affirmations, visualization, and mental imagery.
- Successful bowlers establish process-oriented goals.
- Exercise and nutrition enhance both your physical and mental game.

Assessment 8-1

The Process of Goal Setting

Name _____   Section _____   Date _____

This series of steps provides a process you can use to set and realize a goal.

1. Write a statement of your goal:

   _____

   _____

2. Is it sufficiently specific so you will know when you have reached it? If not, rewrite it:

   _____

   _____

3. Is it positively stated? If not, rewrite it:

   _____

   _____

4. Is it under your control, in that it focuses on your behavior, not someone else's? If not, rewrite it:

   _____

   _____

5. Is it a goal rather than a result? If not, rewrite it:

   _____

   _____

6. Is the goal important enough to you that you want to work on it and have the time and energy?

   _____ Yes _____ No

   If not, rewrite it:

   _____

   _____

7. How will reaching this goal make your life different?

   _____

   _____

8. What barriers might you encounter in working toward the goal?
   Knowledge roadblock. What more do I need to know?

   _____

   _____

   Skill roadblock. What more must I learn how to do?

   _____

   _____

Risk-taking roadblock. What risks must I take? _____

_____

Social support roadblock. From whom do I need support? What kind of support is it? _____

_____

9. Goal plan: identify the steps you need to take to achieve the goal. One way to do
this is to use a *ladder approach* to write down the steps in reverse order.
Assessment 8-2 demonstrates how this is done.

Assessment 8-2

Using the Goal Ladder

Name _____ Section _____ Date _____

In conceptualizing the steps it takes to achieve a goal, it often helps to use a *ladder approach,* writing down the steps in reverse order. Step 1 is at the bottom of the ladder, and the final step is at the top. Make sure the steps you identify are small and manageable. If they are not, divide them until they are. Here is an example you can use for your ladder approach. Of course, it's fine if it takes more than 10 steps to reach your goal.

Goal: _____

_____

_____

_____

10. _____

_____

9. _____

_____

8. _____

_____

7. _____

_____

6. _____

_____

5. _____

_____

4. _____

_____

3. _____

_____

2. _____

_____

1. _____

_____

Assessment 8-3

Your Master Plan to Winning

Name   Section   Date

Physical Game	Equipment	Lane Play	Mental Game

Here's how to use this table to establish your master plan for winning:

1. Mark down what you need to work on to improve your physical game in the Physical Game column.

2. List your equipment and what type of lane conditions it is used for, or describe an extra bowling ball you need to complement the one(s) you already own, in the Equipment column.

3. Describe ideal lane conditions and the lane conditions where you experience the most difficulty in the Lane Play column. Concentrate your mental effort and your physical practice schedule on lane conditions where you are weak.

4. Identify if you need to relax and slow down or become more aroused and speed up in the Mental Game column. Engineer a mental game that will help you achieve your optimal arousal level.

CHAPTER 9

HOW TO **STRENGTHEN YOUR GAME:**
WARM-UP AND CONDITIONING

OBJECTIVES

After reading this chapter, you should be able to do the following:

- Explain the importance of warm-up exercises.
- Perform basic warm-up exercises to prevent injury.
- Perform neck, shoulder, and lower body warm-up exercises.

KEY TERM

While reading this chapter, you will become familiar with the following terms:

▶ **Microtrauma**

BASIC WARM-UP EXERCISES TO PREVENT INJURY

If people viewed bowling as a sport requiring proper strength and conditioning, the number of bowling-related injuries would probably be significantly reduced. Although some injuries are caused by accidents, many others are the result of strain and stress on the body that builds up over time. An injury caused by strain and stress is referred to as **microtrauma.** In bowling, microtrauma builds up in your shoulders, elbows, wrists, and hands.

The principal cause of microtrauma is lack of prebowling warm-up exercises. Performing some simple warm-up exercises just before you bowl limbers your muscles and joints, prepares your body for maximum physical performance, and helps prevent injury.

The following loosening-up exercises are designed especially to limber those areas of your body that you use most when you bowl. We recommend performing three sets of five repetitions for each exercise. The exercises are most effective when you perform them once or twice daily, and especially just before you bowl.

QUADRICEPS

This warm-up exercise stretches the muscles in the front of your legs. Figure 9-1 shows how to do it.

1. Balance on one leg while grasping the foot of your other leg.
2. Now stretch your leg back to your opposite buttock. Hold this position for at least 20 seconds.
3. Perform five repetitions and then repeat the warm-up with your other leg.

FIGURE 9-1
Quadriceps warm-up.

FIGURE 9-2 Triceps warm-up.

TRICEPS

This warm-up exercise limbers your triceps. Figure 9-2 shows how it is performed.
1. Lift the elbow of one arm over your head while lowering the rest of your arm behind your back.
2. Grasp your elbow with your other hand, and pull it gently toward the middle of your head.
3. Do five repetitions, and then repeat the warm-up with your other arm.

FOREARM EXTENSORS AND FLEXORS

Forearm extensors and flexors are warm-up exercises to prepare your forearms for bowling.

► Extensors

Figure 9-3 shows how to do a forearm extensor warm-up.
1. Extend your arm with your hand bent down at the wrist.
2. Grasp the fingers of your hand with your other hand.
3. Pull your fingers gently toward your body.
4. Do five repetitions, and then repeat the warm-up with your other arm.

FIGURE 9-3 Forearm extensor warm-up.

► Microtrauma
An injury caused by strain and stress. In bowling, microtrauma builds up in your shoulders, elbows, wrists, and hands.

▶ **Flexors**

Figure 9-4 shows how to perform a forearm flexor warm-up exercise.

1. Extend your arm with the palm of your hand facing out and your hand bent upward at the wrist.
2. Grasp the fingers of your extended hand with your other hand.
3. Gently pull the fingers toward your body.
4. Do five repetitions and then repeat the warm-up with your other arm.

FIGURE 9-4 Forearm flexor warm-up.

NECK, SHOULDER, AND LOWER BODY WARM-UPS

These warm-up exercises limber up the muscles in your neck, shoulders, and lower body.

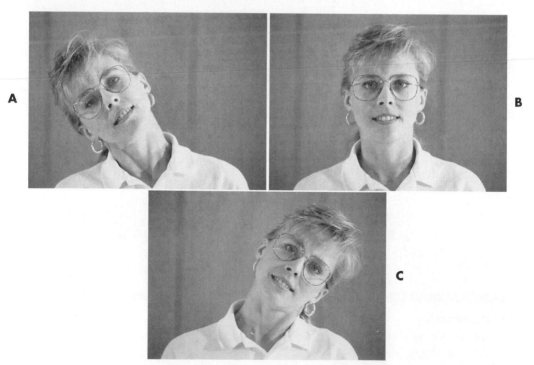

FIGURE 9-5 Neck and shoulder stretch.

▶ Neck and Shoulder Stretch

Figure 9-5 shows how to perform the neck and shoulder stretch warm-up.
1. Look straight ahead.
2. Lean your head to the right.
3. Return to the straight position.
4. Lean your head to the left.
5. Do five repetitions of this warm-up.

▶ Neck Stretch

Figure 9-6 shows how to perform the neck stretch warm-up.
1. Move your chin toward your Adam's apple until you can feel tension on the back of your neck (Figure 9-6, *A*).
2. Hold your chin in that position for 3 to 5 seconds.
3. Release the tension, and repeat the warm-up four more times (Figure 9-6, *B*).

▶ Calf Stretch

The calf stretch warm-up limbers your calf muscles. Figure 9-7 shows how to perform the calf stretch warm-up.
1. Balance the balls of your feet on a stair (or step to the approach).
2. Lower and raise your body using your ankle as a fulcrum.
3. Do five repetitions of this warm-up.

▶ Side Stretch

Side stretches limber your lower back muscles and sides. Figure 9-8 shows how to do this warm-up.
1. Assume a relaxed standing position with your legs spread at a comfortable distance.
2. Extend your right arm over your head while keeping your other arm at your side.

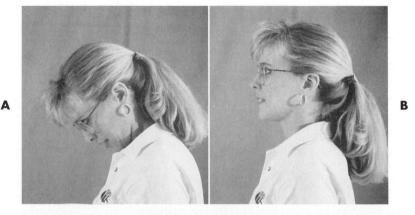

FIGURE 9-6 Neck stretch.

FIGURE 9-7 Calf stretch.

FIGURE 9-8 Side stretch.

FIGURE 9-9 Knee and thigh stretch.

3. Bend sideways at the waist toward your left side until you feel a slight tension on the back muscles on your right side. Hold the position for 20 seconds.
4. Do five repetitions, and then repeat the warm-up with your left arm.

▶ Knee and Thigh Stretch

This warm-up exercise limbers your knees and thighs. Figure 9-9 shows how to perform this warm-up.
1. Place your left leg in back and your right leg in front of your body.
2. Shift the weight of your body forward, bending your right knee as you do so.
3. Hold this position for about 5 seconds.
4. Do five repetitions of this warm-up, shift legs, and do five more.

▶ Achilles Stretch

This warm-up exercise stretches your Achilles tendons. Figure 9-10 shows how it is performed.
1. Place the palms of your hands against a wall.
2. Position your left leg in back and your right leg in front of your body at a comfortable position.
3. Stretch out your left leg while you bend your right knee until you feel tension.
4. Hold this position for about 5 seconds.
5. Relax and then repeat the warm-up four more times.
6. Shift your leg positions and do five repetitions.

FIGURE 9-10 Achilles stretch.

FIGURE 9-11 Toe touches.

▶ **Toe Touch**

The toe touches limbers your lumbar muscles and stretches your leg muscles. Figure 9-11 shows how this warm-up is performed.

1. From a standing position, cross your legs.
2. Bend your body at the waist, and try to place your fingers on your toes.
3. When you reach a point where you cannot bend further, hold for about 3 to 5 seconds.
4. Relax and straighten up.
5. Do four more repetitions.
6. Shift your legs and do five repetitions.

SUMMARY

- Warm-up exercises are necessary to prevent bowling-related injuries and micro-trauma.
- Warm-up exercises for bowlers include exercises for every part of the body.

CHAPTER 10

BOWLING LEAGUES AND TOURNAMENTS:
TODAY AND IN THE FUTURE

OBJECTIVES

After reading this chapter, you should be able to do the following:

- Define and briefly describe the purpose of leagues and tournaments.
- Identify and describe the various types of leagues and tournaments and how you can participate in them.
- Explain the purpose of the handicap system.
- Describe the two handicap systems currently in use.

KEY TERMS

While reading this chapter, you will become familiar with the following terms:

▶ ABC

▶ Bracket Tournament

▶ Couples' Leagues

▶ Division

▶ Handicap System

▶ Handicap Tournament

▶ Mixed Leagues

▶ Sanctioned Leagues *Continued*

KEY TERMS

- ▶ Sanctioned Tournament
- ▶ Scratch Tournaments
- ▶ Special Interest Leagues
- ▶ WIBC
- ▶ YABA

LEAGUES AND TOURNAMENTS

The **ABC** (American Bowling Congress), **WIBC** (Women's International Bowling Congress), and **YABA** (Young American Bowling Alliance) coordinate league activities at thousands of bowling centers throughout the United States. Leagues organized by these national associations are called **sanctioned leagues.** You should investigate leagues in your area and join one.

In addition to sanctioned league competition, there is **sanctioned tournament** competition. These tournaments are organized at the local, state, and national levels. There are different tournaments for different classes of bowlers, so even beginners can enjoy the thrill of one-on-one competition in a tournament.

Because of the **handicap system** used by leagues, new bowlers can compete successfully in any sanctioned league. The handicap system provides newer bowlers having lower averages with a head start by giving them handicap points before the game even starts.

There are also tournaments that give lower averaging bowlers handicap points so they can compete with bowlers whose averages are far higher.

▶ **ABC**
American Bowling Congress. The official governing body for men's league bowling.

▶ **WIBC**
Women's International Bowling Congress. The national governing body for women's league bowling.

▶ **YABA**
Young American Bowling Alliance. Coordinates youth league competition, trains coaches, and develops educational programs for public schools and colleges.

▶ **Sanctioned Leagues**
Bowling leagues governed by the rules and regulations of a national bowling organization.

▶ **Sanctioned Tournament**
A bowling tournament that is governed by the rules and regulations of a national bowling organization.

▶ **Handicap System**
A process by which points are given to teams or individual bowlers that helps equalize the scores of the teams or bowlers.

Another form of tournament is the **bracket tournament.** Bracket tournaments group bowlers with averages falling within a range or bracket. For example, all bowlers having averages ranging between 130 and 145 would compete against each other.

JOINING A LEAGUE

To join a league, call your local bowling center. Someone at the control desk will be able to assist you. Fall and winter leagues usually start around Labor Day and continue for about 12 to 36 weeks. Summer leagues run from May to August.

Almost all the tedious work is handled by the league secretary. The league secretary keeps all personal and team records, calculates averages and handicaps each week, schedules the teams you will play, assigns lanes, and posts team and individual standings within the league. All this information is posted on the bowling center's league bulletin board. All you have to do is show up each week, check the bulletin board, pay your dues, and bowl the best you can!

CHOOSING THE LEAGUE THAT'S RIGHT FOR YOU

Don't join a league hastily. Do some research first. Make sure you are teamed with people whose company you will enjoy. The best way to obtain the information about a league is to ask someone at the control desk or the bowling center's proprietor. They will steer you in the right direction. After all, the bowling center proprietor really has one goal: to make sure you enjoy yourself and keep coming back.

For single people, there are **mixed leagues;** for couples there are **couples' leagues;** and there are numerous men's and women's leagues. There are also many **special interest leagues** you might want to consider joining. These include senior citizens', career/vocational, and local school leagues. In special interest leagues you know you will be in the company of those who share common interests with you.

Another point to consider is how evenly you are matched with the other bowlers in the league. You need to make sure that you are matched as closely as possible to those who have equal bowling abilities. Most bowling centers have one or more leagues made up of top-notch bowlers. Even though extra handicap points will help you, you probably won't enjoy bowling a 120 game when others around you are bowling 180 or better. Ask around the bowling center, and find out which leagues are for newer players.

Also, make sure you get along well with your team members. Nothing can ruin the fun of bowling more than conflict between teammates. The safest bet is to talk some of your friends into joining the league with you and form your own team.

Above all, don't feel self-conscious about having a low average when you begin league competition. The lower your average, the more handicap points you will receive. Also, as a new player, you will improve much faster than seasoned members. These two factors will make you a real asset to your team.

THE GREAT EQUALIZER: THE HANDICAP SYSTEM

As discussed, league competition is based on a handicap system. The handicap system *spots* extra points to bowlers with lower averages. Let's investigate the handicap system a bit further.

When you bowl on a league, your average score is calculated by the league secretary each week. As you might suspect, your average is the running total of all your scores divided by the number of games you have bowled in the league so far. This means that if you start bowling better each week, your average will go up. When you start a new season, your beginning average is the average you had for the previous year. The accompanying box shows some examples of averages.

A handicap is based on a percentage of the difference between your team average and the average of the other team. This percentage is usually between 70% and

Calculating Averages

Your average is the running total of all your scores divided by the number of games you have bowled so far.

Example 1

Game 1	152
Game 2	137
Game 3	141
Game 4	128
TOTAL	551

Average = 137.75 or 138

Example 2

Game 1	147
Game 2	139
Game 3	165
Game 4	160
Game 5	132
Game 6	116
Game 7	127
TOTAL	986

Average = 140.85 or 141

▶ **Bracket Tournament**
A tournament in which bowlers who have the same range of average scores compete with one another.

▶ **Mixed Leagues**
Leagues in which single men and women bowl.

▶ **Couples' Leagues**
Leagues in which couples (married, engaged, or just friends) bowl.

▶ **Special Interest Leagues**
Leagues that cater to individuals having a common interest, such as teachers, senior citizens, or professionals.

90%. In the following example, we will use the 90% handicap system to calculate handicaps.

Let's assume that you are a member of a team having five players. (A team can have between two and five players.) The box below at left shows the statistics for your team.

Your team's total average is 140 + 130 + 120 + 115 + 135, or 640.

Team USA, the official bowling team representing the United States, happens to be in town and wants to play your team in their first exhibition game! The box below at right shows the statistics on Team USA.

Note that the two strongest bowlers occupy the first and last positions of the team. This is how teams field their players. It's similar to a baseball hitting line-up; the first bowler tries to start the frame with a show of strength, and then the last bowler acts as the clean up person.

Statistics for Your Team		Statistics for Team USA	
Player No.	Average	Player No.	Average
1	140	1	225
2	130	2	210
3	120	3	215
4	115	4	210
5	135	5	220

Team USA's total average is 225 + 210 + 215 + 210 + 220, or 1080.

Using the 90% handicap system, we multiply the difference in averages by 90% to determine your team's handicap:

$$1080 - 640 = 440$$

$$440 \times 90\% = 396$$

Your handicap is 396 points (or pins). This means that even before you begin the game, your team starts with a head start of 396 points (or pins). The starting score will be: Your Team, 396; Team USA, 0.

So, you can see why handicaps are the great equalizer in bowling.

TOURNAMENTS

Sanctioned ABC/WIBC tournaments are a great way to enjoy the thrill of one-on-one competition. The three basic types of tournaments you can compete in are handicap, scratch, and bracket.

The tournament doesn't have to be a national or state tournament to offer top prizes, sometimes thousands of dollars. Even local tournaments offer these prizes. If you decide to compete in a state or national tournament, you are eligible to win the cash prizes and also get the opportunity to travel, see new places, and meet people who share a common interest in bowling.

HANDICAP TOURNAMENTS

In a **handicap tournament,** you may receive bonus pins based on the difference between your bowling average and your opponent's bowling average or the difference between your average and 210 points. Here's how it works.

▶ Calculating Based on Averages

Suppose you have an average of 150 and the person you are bowling against has an average of 190. The difference between the two averages is 40 pins. If this is a 90% handicap tournament, you are spotted 36 pins before the match begins.

▶ Calculating Based on 210 Points

Assuming that your average is still 150, the difference between your average and 210 is calculated, giving 60 points. Your handicap is 90% of the difference (60 x .90), or 54 points; 54 points is added to each game you bowl.

A handicap tournament is a great opportunity for new bowlers to win. As a new bowler, it is much easier for you to make a couple of extra strikes and bowl 100 points over your average than it is for a bowler having a 200 average to bowl 100 points over his or her average.

SCRATCH TOURNAMENTS

Scratch tournaments have no handicaps. The final score at the end of the game is all that counts.

▶ **Handicap Tournament**
Tournament in which handicaps are assigned to the participating bowlers.

▶ **Scratch Tournaments**
Tournaments in which no handicaps are assigned. Each bowler competes using his or her actual scores.

BRACKET TOURNAMENTS

In bracket tournaments, you only compete against those whose averages are close to yours. You bowl within a **division** of bowlers with similar averages. An example of a bracket tournament division would be a 110-115 division, which means all bowlers having averages between 110 and 115 points compete against each other.

Some bracket tournaments are open to only those who have a certain average. For example, there are tournaments for bowlers whose averages are greater than 180. Conversely, there are tournaments for bowlers whose averages are less than 180.

Get involved; join a league at your local bowling center and see what it's all about. Consider competing in a tournament. These interesting and wholesome activities broaden your bowling experiences and help you decide how far you want to go in this great sport.

SUMMARY

- Leagues and tournaments are sanctioned events that allow you to bowl competitively with other bowlers according to universally recognized rules.
- Sanctioned leagues are governed by national organizations in which you can participate. You can join many different types of leagues to enjoy the sport of bowling.
- Tournaments are organized at local, state, and national levels that allow bowlers to compete one-on-one with each other. Anyone can enter a tournament regardless of their average score.
- Bowling handicaps allow new bowlers to compete successfully in any sanctioned league because the handicap serves as a score equalizer.
- Two handicap systems are used to determine bowling handicaps: calculation based on averages and calculation based on a percentage of the difference between your average and your competition's average.

▶ **Division**
Term used in bracket tournaments to define the range of averages of the competitors.

APPENDIX

BOWLING **RULES**

Introduction

The rules of bowling are relatively standard, regardless of the sanctioning organization. The rules in this appendix are a condensed version of the American Bowling Congress (ABC) and Women's International Bowling Congress (WIBC) rules. To include the rules in their entirety would make this book too long! Your bowling center can provide a complete rule book.

Rule 1: Leagues and Tournaments

Leagues and tournaments must be organized and bowled in accordance with the WIBC bylaws/ABC constitution, rules, and regulations. These events must be scheduled on lanes that are currently WIBC/ABC certified, and only WIBC/ABC–approved equipment may be used.

Rule 2: Game: Definition

A game of American tenpins consists of 10 frames. A player delivers two balls in each of the first nine frames unless a strike is scored. In the tenth frame a player delivers three balls if a strike or spare is scored. Every frame must be completed by each player bowling in regular order.

Rule 4a: Legal Delivery

A delivery is made when the ball leaves the player's possession and crosses the foul line into playing territory. Every delivery counts unless a dead ball is declared. A delivery must be made entirely by manual means. No device may be incorporated in or affixed to the ball that detaches on delivery or is a moving part during delivery except as provided in rules 4b and 4c.

Rule 4b: Special Equipment to Grip the Ball

A player may use special equipment to aid in grasping and delivering the ball if it is in place of a hand or major portion thereof lost by amputation or otherwise.

Rule 4c: Mechanical Aids to Grip the Ball

Permission to use special equipment necessary to grasp and deliver the ball because of other disability may be granted as follows:
1. A description or drawing and model of the aid is submitted to WIBC/ABC.
2. A doctor's certificate is furnished to WIBC/ABC, describing the disability and recommending that the aid should be used.
3. The aid does not incorporate a mechanical device with moving parts that would impart a force or impetus to the ball.
4. Permission to use the aid is given by each league or tournament the player enters.
   When authorization is given, the player will be provided with a special card stating that the use of the specified mechanical aid has been approved by WIBC/ABC. If permission is

not granted, the player has the right of appeal to the WIBC or ABC legal committee. Permission to use the device may be withdrawn for cause.

Rule 5a: Definition of a Foul

A foul occurs when a part of the player's body encroaches on or goes beyond the foul line and touches any part of the lane, equipment, or building during or after a delivery. A ball is in play after a delivery until the same or another player is on the approach in position to make a succeeding delivery.

The certification and inspection committee of a local association can require that the foul line be plainly marked on the walls, posts, division boards, or any other structure in a bowling center on a line with the regular foul line.

Rule 5c: Foul Counts as Ball Bowled

When a foul is recorded, the delivery counts but the player is not credited with any pins knocked down by that delivery. Pins knocked down by the ball when the foul occurred must be respotted if the player who fouled is entitled to additional deliveries in the frame.

Rule 6a: Legal Pin Fall

Pins to be credited to a player following a legal delivery include the following:
1. Pins knocked down or off the pin deck by the ball or another pin.
2. Pins knocked down or off the pin deck by a pin rebounding from a side partition or rear cushion.
3. Pins knocked down or off the pin deck by a pin rebounding from the sweep bar when it is at rest on the pin deck before sweeping dead wood from the pin deck.
4. Pins that lean and touch the kickback or side partition. All such pins are termed dead wood and must be removed before the next delivery. No pins may be conceded and only pins actually knocked down or moved entirely off the playing surface of the lane as a result of a legal delivery may be counted.

Rule 6b: Illegal Pin Fall

When any of the following occurs, the delivery counts but the resulting pin fall does not:
1. A ball leaves the lane before reaching the pins.
2. A ball rebounds from the rear cushion.
3. A pin rebounds after coming in contact with the body, arms, or legs of a human pinsetter.
4. A pin is touched by mechanical pin-setting equipment.
5. Any pin is knocked down when dead wood is being removed.
6. Any pin is knocked down by a human pinsetter.
7. The player commits a foul.
8. A delivery is made with dead wood on the lane or in the gutter, and the ball contacts such dead wood before leaving the lane surface.

If illegal pin fall occurs and the player is entitled to additional deliveries in the frame, the pin or pins illegally knocked down must be respotted where they originally stood before delivery of the ball.

Rule 11: Forfeit: Delay of Game

No unreasonable delay in the progress of any game is permitted. If a player or team in a league or tournament refuses to proceed with a game after being directed to do so by a league or tournament official, the game or series shall be declared forfeited.

Rule 18: Bowling Ball: Private Ownership

A bowling ball is considered the property of the owner. A player is prohibited from using another player's ball without the owner's consent.

Rule 19: Bowling Ball: Altering Surface

Altering the surface of a bowling ball by the use of abrasives while bowling in sanctioned competition is prohibited. All bowling balls so altered must be removed from the competition.

NOTE: If it is shown the bowler had prior knowledge her/his actions were in violation of rule 19, the game in which the violation occurred is subject to forfeiture. In addition, the bowler is subject to dismissal from the league and suspension of membership.

Competition is defined as the remainder of the current game and remaining game(s) in the series being bowled. The use of approved cleaning agents such as isopropyl (rubbing) alcohol and polishing machines is permissible.

Rule 51: ABC Individual Awards

A member is eligible for one award in each of the following categories during an ABC fiscal year (August 1–July 31):
1. Single game score of 300
2. Single game score of 299
3. Single game score of 298
4. Eleven (11) strikes in a row, starting in frame one, when the score is 297 or less
5. Eleven (11) strikes in a row, starting in frame two; single game score 100 pins over game average
6. Three-game series totaling 700 to 799
7. Three-game series totaling 800 to 899

A member is eligible for one award in a lifetime for a three-game series totaling 900. Where a choice of awards is available in any category the member is entitled to a choice of an award for the first score recorded. Any additional score in the same category that fiscal year will be officially recognized by ABC but will not qualify for an award.

Rule 52: ABC Series Awards

When more than three, but less than six, games are bowled in series, only the first three games count for three-game series awards. If six or more games are bowled in a series, each succeeding set of three games, following the first three games, shall qualify as a separate series.

To qualify for the three-game series award, the series of games can be bowled consecutively against one or more opponents on the same scheduled date in a league or a squad in a tournament.

Rule 53: ABC Fiscal Year Awards

During each fiscal year, ending July 31, the following recognition awards will be made by ABC to the sponsors of two-, three-, four-, and five-man and mixed teams that bowl one of the three highest scores in the nation in each of the following classifications:

1. Three-game series total
2. Single team game score

Awards are also made to a member who bowls one of the three highest scores in a three game series.

No individual or sponsor is entitled to receive more than one fiscal year award in each category. An individual or sponsor qualifying more than once during a fiscal year will receive recognition only for the highest award in that category.

Rule 54: ABC Inspection and Reporting Procedures

When any of the following scores are bowled: 300, 299, 298 games; an 800 or better by an individual in a three-game series, or single-game and three-game series team scores above the accompanying figures:

	Game	Series
5-player	1250	3600
4-player	750	2800
3-player	750	2200
2-player	525	1500

these procedures apply:

1. The league or tournament secretary shall notify the local association secretary or authorized representative within 48 hours and submit a completed high score award application within 20 days.
2. The association secretary or authorized representative shall submit a completed high score application to ABC as soon as possible but not more than 30 days after the score was bowled.

Failure to comply with any of the foregoing shall be grounds for denial of ABC high score recognition. If an award cannot be approved administratively, the applicant will be notified in writing, setting forth the reasons for denial. If within 15 days of receipt of the written notice the applicant files a written appeal, the claim will be submitted for final decision to the ABC High Score and Awards Review Committee.

NOTE: The above procedures are in effect until such time as a fourth decision of noncompliance occurs. At that time ABC/WIBC will notify center management and league and tour-

nament officials that when any of the above scores are bowled, the lanes must be inspected
for compliance in keeping with the procedures outlined in article 16, item f, of the ABC constitution.

Rule 55b: ABC Special Awards

Awards will be provided for the following:
1. Conversion of the 7-10 split
2. Conversion of the 4-6-7-10 split
3. All-spare game
4. Dutch 200 game
5. Three consecutive games of the same score in a series
6. 150 pins over average in a three-game series

A member shall be entitled to receive the 150 pins over average in a three-game series award
even though the series may qualify for an award in the ABC individual awards category.

Rule 50: WIBC Awards Eligibility

WIBC will recognize the accomplishments of WIBC members participating in WIBC-sanc-
tioned leagues and tournaments, as indicated in this appendix.

To qualify for recognition, all provisions of the WIBC bylaws, specifications, and rules
must have been met at the time the score was bowled. The provisions of these rules shall also
apply to play-offs for ties in leagues and tournaments.

Rule 52: WIBC National All-Women and Mixed Team Recognition

Recognition will be provided to members bowling their first 298, 299, and 300 games and
first three-game series of 800 and over each season. A member is eligible for recognition of
one three-game series totaling 900 each season.

Each season, WIBC will recognize the sponsors and members of five-, four-, three-, and
two-player and mixed teams that bowl one of the three highest scores in the congress in
each of the following classifications:
1. Three-game series total of 3425 (five-woman), 2750 (four-woman), 2075 (three-woman),
   and 1350 (two-woman). Three-game series total of 3600 (five-player), 2800 (four-
   player), 2200 (three-player), and 1500 (two-player) for mixed team recognition.
2. Single team game scores of 1175 (five-woman), 950 (four-woman), 725 (three-woman),
   and 500 (two-woman). Single team game scores of 1250 (five-player), 1000 (four-
   player), 750 (three-player), and 525 (two-player) for mixed team recognition.

No individual or sponsor is entitled to receive more than one award in each award classification. An individual or sponsor qualifying more than once during a fiscal year will receive recognition only for the highest award in that classification.

To be eligible for recognition of these accomplishments, the scores are to be reported by the
secretary of the league or tournament to the local association secretary. The local association
secretary is to submit a completed superior performance recognition application to WIBC.

In the event a score cannot be recognized administratively, the bowler will be notified in
writing of the reasons for denying the award. If a written appeal is filed within 15 days of re-

ceipt of the notice, the claim will be submitted for a final decision to a committee acting for and in behalf of the WIBC board of directors.

Rule 53: WIBC High Score Recognition (275-297 Game, 500 and 600 Series)

WIBC will recognize the first game of 275 to 297 bowled by a member each season. In addition, recognition will be given to members bowling their first three-game series of 500 through 599 and 600 through 699 each season.

The following provisions apply to the recognition of 500 and 600 series:

1. A member with a 140 average and below shall be eligible for the 500 through 599 recognition.
2. A member with a 170 average and below shall be eligible for the 600 through 699 series recognition.
3. If a member is eligible for the 500 and 600 awards and bowls a 600 series before a 500 series, she is eligible for the 600 award and is no longer eligible for the 500 award.

To determine average categories, the following shall apply:

League Play

1. If 21 games or more have been bowled in the league in the current season, use the current average.
2. If games have not yet been bowled in the current season, use the final average for 21 games or more from the preceding season in the same league.
3. For a new bowler in the league, if 21 games have not yet been bowled in the current season, use the previous season's highest average for 21 games or more in any sanctioned league.
4. In a summer league, when a bowler has not established an average in the previous season, her highest average of 21 games or more from the regular season just completed shall be used. In a regular league, when a bowler has not established an average in the previous season, her highest average of 21 games or more from the summer league just completed shall be used.
5. A new bowler in the league who has not bowled 21 games in the current season and does not have an acceptable average for comparison is not eligible for recognition.

Tournament Play

1. In handicap or classified tournaments, compare the score with the average used in the tournament.
2. In scratch tournaments, compare the score with the bowler's highest current average of 21 games or more. If 21 games have not been bowled in the current season, compare the score with the previous season's highest average for 21 games or more. A bowler who does not have an acceptable average for comparison is not eligible for recognition.

Rule 56: WIBC Pins Over Average Recognition

Game

Recognition will be given to WIBC members who bowl 75 or 100 pins over average in a single game. If a bowler qualifies for 75 and 100 pins over average recognition for a single game, she is only eligible for 100 pins over average recognition.

Series

Pins over average recognition is given to WIBC members who bowl 125 pins over average in a three-game series. The following provisions apply to determine eligibility.

League Play
1. If 21 games or more have been bowled in the league in the current season, compare the score with the current average.
2. If 21 games have not yet been bowled in the current season, compare the score with the final average for 21 games or more from the preceding season in the same league.
3. For a new bowler in the league, if 21 games have not yet been bowled in the current season, compare the score with the previous season's highest average for 21 games or more.
4. In a summer league, when a bowler has not established an average in the previous season, her highest average of 21 games or more from the regular season just completed may be used for comparison. In a regular league, when a bowler has not established an average in the previous season, her highest average of 21 games or more from the summer season just completed may be used for comparison.
5. A new bowler in the league who has not bowled 21 games in the current season and does not have an acceptable average for comparison is not eligible for recognition.

Tournament Play
1. In handicap or classified tournaments, compare the score with the average used in the tournament.
2. In scratch tournaments, compare the score with the bowler's highest current average for 21 games or more. If 21 games have not been bowled in the current season, compare the score with the previous season's highest average for 21 games. A bowler who does not have an acceptable average for comparison is not eligible for recognition.

Rule 59: WIBC Most Improved Bowler

Each league is provided with an award to recognize the WIBC member who shows the greatest improvement in average for the season. The award is to be given to the bowler who is eligible, regardless of how many league awards she is qualified to receive. To qualify for the most improved average award, the following provisions apply, unless otherwise provided by league rule:
1. The member must have bowled at least two thirds of the games scheduled during the league's current season. If a substitute later becomes a regular member of the league, she must bowl the required number of games as a regular member to qualify for the award.
2. Bowler's increase in average is determined by comparing her final average for the current season with her highest final or book average of at least 21 games for the preceding season in the same league.
3. For a new member in the league with an established average, compare her final average for the current season with her highest final or book average, based on at least 21 games, for the preceding season. NOTE: The preceding season for a winter league would be the previous winter season, and for a summer league it would be the previous summer season.
4. For a bowler with no average for the preceding season, compare her final average for

the current season with her average for her first 21games during the current season. In leagues bowling 30 games or less, compare her final average with the average of her first 12 games. When a tie exists, the winner shall be determined on the basis of the percentage of a full pin.

Rule 105a: Legal Line-up

A legal line-up in league play is one of the following:
1. Three or more eligible players in five-player team leagues
2. Two or more eligible players in either three- or four-player team leagues
3. One eligible player in two-player team leagues

A league may include in its rules the number of players from a team's roster who must be present to count toward a legal line-up. Substitutes count to determine a legal line-up unless otherwise provided by league rule.

A five-player team league may adopt a rule that two or more eligible players are required for a legal line-up. A three- or four-player team league may adopt a rule that only one eligible player is required for a legal line-up.

Rule 105b: Absentee and Vacancy

Leagues may adopt rules for absentee or vacancy scores and handicaps to decide league games. Absentee or vacancy scores may be used only when a legal line-up is present. Absentee or vacancy scores may not replace scores bowled by an ineligible player.
1. An absentee score is to be used when a member is absent and a substitute is not available. For the WIBC, handicap must be added to an absentee score in a handicap league. The following provisions apply unless otherwise provided by league rule:
   a. The absentee score for each game shall be the absent member's current average less 10 pins. In handicap leagues the handicap shall be based on the absent member's current average. When there are additional members on a team's roster, the absentee score of the absent member with the most games bowled shall be used. If two absentee scores are needed, the average of the absentee with the next highest number of games shall be used. When two absent members have the same number of games, the lower absentee score shall be used.
   b. When a team has an absent member without an established average, a score of 120 will be used. In handicap leagues the handicap shall be based on the score of 120.
2. A vacancy score is to be used when a team has an incomplete roster. If the vacancy score has not been specified by league rule, it shall be 120. In handicap leagues the handicap must be based on the vacancy score used. For the WIBC, in a singles league no vacancy scores shall be used. Absentee scores will not be permitted, unless otherwise provided by league rule.

Rule 106d: Tardy Players

Unless otherwise provided by league rule, a player who arrives late may be permitted to bowl after a game has started under these conditions:
1. The player shall begin play with the score to count beginning with the frame then being bowled by the team.

2. The player shall receive one tenth of the absentee score for each frame not bowled.
3. Partial games shall not be used in determining a bowler's average unless league rules require the secretary to maintain averages based on the actual frames bowled by each player.

Rule 106e: Bowling Out

A bowler may finish the final game of a series before teammates or opponents, unless league rules do not permit bowling out.

NOTE: A player bowling out should do so while the others continue to bowl. The player should bowl on each lane immediately after the previous bowler completes the frame, so that the progress of the game is not delayed.

Rule 107c: Substitutes or Replacements

A substitute is a bowler who replaces another who is scheduled to participate in a WIBC/ABC–sanctioned league or bowls for a team with an incomplete roster. Scores bowled by a substitute shall count for the games bowled. A substitute must be a member of WIBC/ABC, a local association, and a state association, where required.

The following shall apply to the use of substitutes:

1. A substitute may bowl with any team in the league but may not compete on more than one team in the same league for the regularly scheduled games each week, unless otherwise provided by league rule.
2. The average of a substitute shall be kept. Should a substitute later be added to a team's roster, her or his average shall be continued.
3. Scores bowled through the efforts of more than one individual player shall not qualify for league, WIBC, or ABC individual awards.
4. In mixed leagues, when a substitute or replacement is made for a female (male) bowler, the substitute or replacement must also be a female (male), unless the league made other provisions in its rules.
5. A player removed from a game cannot return to bowl in the same game.
6. Substitutes are not required to pay league fees, unless otherwise provided by league rule.
7. Substitutes are not entitled to attend league meetings.
8. When a substitution is made during a game, as provided in item 9, the game score counts only for team score, unless otherwise provided by league rule.
9. *WIBC:* a captain may replace any player at any time during a game with another eligible player if a bowler is unable to finish the game because of disability, injury, or an emergency. A player may not be replaced during a game for any other reason unless the league adopted a rule granting this privilege. *ABC:* a captain may replace any player at any time during a game with another eligible player unless otherwise provided by league rule.
10. *WIBC:* a team using a substitute is eligible for all high team prizes.

NOTE: When a substitution is made during a game in a handicap league, each player receives 1/10 of her or his single game handicap for each frame bowled.

For example, an original player with a single game handicap of 19 pins completes six frames and a substitute with a single game handicap of 22 pins completes the remaining four:

Original: $\frac{1}{10}$ of 19 = 1. 9 pins x 6 frames =11.4, or 11 pins
Substitute player: $\frac{1}{10}$ of 22 = 2.2 pins x 4 frames = 8.8 pins, or 8 pins

The fraction is dropped from each individual's handicap, not from each frame. In leagues using the team method of handicapping, the same procedure is used. Determine the team handicap with the original player and with the substitute in the line-up. Then apply the handicap based on the number of frames completed by each player.

Rule 111a: Schedules

League games must be bowled as scheduled unless postponed. The board of directors or a committee appointed for this purpose shall determine what is sufficient cause to grant a postponement, but it cannot adopt a rule that would have the effect of not permitting any postponements.

Prebowled games shall be subject to the same conditions that apply to postponed games. *WIBC:* a postponement shall be granted if a team is unable to field a legal line-up because some of its bowlers are participating in the WIBC local or state association tournament or attending the WIBC annual meeting.

Rule 111b: Postponement: Request

A postponement must be requested at least 48 hours before the scheduled time except for emergencies. A league must grant a postponement when a team cannot appear for reasons beyond its control.

Rule 111c: Postponement: Time Limit for Scheduling

Postponed games must be bowled before the final date of scheduled competition for team standings. However, postponements granted for the final date of scheduled competition for team standings must be bowled not later than 7 days after that date.

The foregoing applies except when a protest or appeal is pending finalization under Rule 119.

Rule 111d: Postponement: Procedures to Follow

When a postponement has been granted, the following procedures apply:
1. The league secretary shall notify the bowling center of the change in schedule and arrange to have a pair of acceptable lanes available for the postponed match.
2. The captains of the teams involved shall agree to a date for bowling the postponed match. If within 1 week from the date originally scheduled, the captains cannot agree on a date, the league secretary shall set a date and notify both team captains of the date and time. This notification is to be given at least 3 days before the date set.
3. Postponed games must be bowled under the same conditions and rules governing sanctioned league play. The teams shall oppose each other on the originally scheduled

pair of lanes if available; otherwise, the league secretary may authorize the teams to bowl on any other pair normally used by the league.

4. If a pair of lanes normally used by the league is not available, the league board of directors may authorize the games to be bowled on another pair of certified lanes even though the lanes are not normally used by the league.

Rule 113a: Play-offs

A play-off is necessary under the following conditions:

1. To determine the champion when a tie exists for first place at the end of the league schedule
2. To determine a champion when the league bowls a split season
3. To determine first place when a tie occurs in any segment of a split season
4. When the league decides to break a tie for any other position

A league may establish special play-off rules but under no conditions may the play-off consist of less than one game. In the absence of a league rule, the play-off shall consist of the same number of games and be conducted under the same conditions and rules governing league play during the regular season.

When more than two teams are involved in a play-off, total pins from the play-off shall decide the winner unless otherwise provided in the league rules.

If a tie still exists at the end of the play-off, each team will bowl an additional frame. This frame is to be bowled by each team on the lane where it bowled the final frame of the last game, and it shall be scored like a tenth frame. If the tie is still unbroken, the teams involved will alternate lanes for each additional complete frame needed to break the tie.

Play-off games do not count toward individual averages or special league prizes unless otherwise provided by the league rules. When a play-off is necessary, the league secretary shall arrange to have lanes available.

NOTE: Leagues may not adopt rules to allow total pins for the season or team average to break position-standing ties at the conclusion of the season or at the end of any segment of a split season schedule. When an extra frame must be bowled, 1/10 of the handicap for one game shall be given for the extra game.

Rule 115b: Dismissal: Nonpayment of Fees or Improper Withdrawal

When a league member is accused of failing to pay league fees or withdrawing without sufficient cause, the league must try to resolve the matter. A complaint shall be submitted, in writing, to a league officer, and the league shall proceed as follows:

1. Within 1 week after receipt of the written complaint, the president should schedule a meeting of the league board of directors, and the board shall be notified. The meeting should be held at the earliest possible date.
2. Written notice and a copy of the complaint shall be provided to the member or members charged. Such notice should be sent by first class mail or be hand delivered and shall notify the member of the date, time, and place of the meeting, as well as of her or his right to attend and offer a defense.
3. A roster shall be prepared listing those present and absent. A quorum of the board of directors must be present at the meeting.

4. Minutes of the meeting and all documents relating to the charges must be maintained. An accounting must be made of any arrearage, including dates and amounts, whether the accused was present or absent when the arrearage occurred, and the date of replacement.
5. A two-thirds vote of the board members present and voting shall be required to determine if the accused is guilty. If found not guilty, the charges are to be dismissed. If found guilty, the local association is to be furnished with a copy of the following:
    a. The meeting notices
    b. The meeting minutes
    c. The league rules
    d. A record of the accounting developed at the meeting and all supporting documents and materials
    e. The vote count for the recommendation of the league board

In the WIBC these items should be submitted within 7 days. In the ABC, when the defendant is an ABC member, all of the items indicated above must be furnished to the local men's association within 30 days after the meeting.

On receipt of the file, the local association secretary shall verify that complete information was provided and submit a copy of the file to WIBC/ABC. WIBC/ABC will notify the member charged that she or he has 30 days to either pay the money or request a hearing on the charge by submitting a written request to WIBC/ABC. When a hearing is requested, WIBC/ABC will direct the local association to handle the complaint in accordance with the suspension and reinstatement procedures outlined in the *WIBC Bylaws Book* or the *ABC Constitution Book.* One or more of the league officers who attended the meeting of the league board is to appear at the local association hearing.

If the member does not request a hearing, the file will be submitted to the legal committee for a final decision.

Rule 116a: Scoring

In league play, scores must be recorded on a score sheet in plain view of opposing players. Every frame bowled by each player shall be recorded. Each team shall also record the scores of each game in a score book kept by the team captain or someone appointed by the captain for this purpose.

The score sheet is the official record, and the team score books must agree with the score sheet at the end of each game. After the score books are verified and signed by the opposing team captains, these are the league's official record for the season.

Errors in scoring or calculation must be corrected by a league official immediately on discovery. Any questionable errors in scoring or calculation shall be decided by the league board.

Rule 118a: Average: How Determined

A bowling average is determined by dividing the total number of pins credited to a bowler in one sanctioned league by the number of games bowled in that league in a season. Extra pins or fractions must be disregarded in using averages for handicapping or classification purposes. Extra pins or fractions shall be reduced to a percentage of a pin only for the purpose of deciding individual position standings in a league.

Highest average is the best average in one of several sanctioned leagues in which a player competes in one season. *Composite average* is the average of a bowler who bowls in two or more sanctioned leagues in a season. The average is determined by adding the total pins for all of the leagues and dividing the result by the total number of games bowled in those leagues.

Rule 118b: Average: How Established

Each league shall adopt a rule to determine the number of games required to establish an average in that league. When establishing an average, a right-handed bowler must always bowl right-handed. Similarly, a left-handed bowler must always bowl left-handed.

No combination of scores bowled both right- and left-handed can be used to compute an average. The penalty is forfeiture of the game.

Rule 119: Protest Procedures

A protest involving eligibility or playing rules must be confirmed in writing to a league officer, the local association, or WIBC/ABC not later than 15 days after the series in which the infraction occurred is bowled. If a written protest is not filed within that time, the series stands.

A protest resulting from competition in the final 2 weeks of a league schedule must be filed within 48 hours of the final date of the league schedule or the end of a segment if the league bowls a split season.

A protest involving league play-off games must be filed within 48 hours. Each protest must be specific in itself and cannot be construed to cover any prior violation.

An appeal from a decision on a protest must be filed in writing:

1. Within 15 days of notification
2. Within 48 hours when notification occurs in the final 2 weeks of the league schedule or after the league schedule has ended
3. Within 48 hours when notification occurs as a result of play-off competition

Prizes for positions involved cannot be distributed until the protest or appeal is resolved.

Equipment Specifications: Bowling Ball

Approval

Bowling balls used in sanctioned competition shall:

1. Meet ABC/WIBC equipment specifications at time of manufacture
2. Be ABC/WIBC approved
3. Meet the following ABC/WIBC specifications

Material

A bowling ball shall be constructed without voids in its interior, be of a nonmetallic composition material, and conform to the specifications for weight, size, and balance.

The use of minute reflective particles or flakes for decorative purposes shall be permitted in a bowling ball provided such particles or flakes are made a part of the ball at time of manufacture; such particles are evenly distributed in a uniform pattern under a transparent shell at least ¼ inch beneath the surface of the ball so as to have no effect on the balance; and the total amount of such material does not exceed ½ ounce per ball.

Weight, Size, Markings, and Holes

The circumference of a ball shall not be more than 27 inches nor shall it weigh more than 16 pounds. The diameter of the ball must be constant.

The surface of a ball must be free of all depressions or grooves of specific pattern, except for holes or indentations used for gripping the ball, identification letters and numbers, and incidental chipping or marring caused by wear.

The following limitations govern drilling holes in a ball:
1. Holes or indentations, not to exceed five, for gripping purposes
2. One hole for balance purposes, not to exceed 1¼ inch in diameter
3. One vent hole to each finger and thumb hole, not to exceed ¼ inch in diameter
4. One mill hole for inspection purposes, not to exceed ⅝ inch in diameter and ⅛ inch in depth

Balance

After drilling, the following tolerances are allowed in the balance of the ball:
1. For a ball weighing 10 pounds or more
   a. Not more than 3 ounces difference between the top of ball (finger hole side) and the bottom (solid side opposite finger holes)
   b. Not more than 1 ounce difference between the sides to the right and left of the finger holes or between the sides in front of and back of the finger holes
2. For a ball weighing more than 8 pounds but less than 10 pounds
   a. Not more than 2 ounces difference between the top of the ball and the bottom
   b. Not more than ¾ ounce difference between the sides to the right and left or between the front and back of the finger holes
3. For a ball weighing less than 8 pounds
   a. Not more than ¾ ounce difference between the top of the ball and the bottom
   b. Not more than ¾ ounce difference between the sides to the right and left or between the front and back of the finger holes

Other Requirements

Movable devices are not permitted in a ball except that a device for changing the finger span or the size of finger and thumb holes may be inserted, providing the device is locked in position during delivery and cannot be removed from the ball without destroying the device.

Removable devices shall be permitted, provided the following:
1. Such devices are used for changing the span, pitch, or size of the gripping holes.
2. They are constructed of a nonmetallic material.
3. They are locked in position during delivery.
4. No device shall be employed for the purpose of adjusting the static balance of the ball.
5. No voids shall be permitted under the device. All such devices must first be submitted and approved by ABC/WIBC before being used in sanctioned competition. Once approved, the device may not be altered and may not be used in conjunction with any other approved device.

The introduction of metal or any other substance not comparable to the original material used in the manufacture of the ball is prohibited. Also, altering a ball in any way to increase its weight or cause it to be out of balance beyond the tolerances is prohibited.

Plugs may be inserted for the purpose of redrilling a ball. Designs may be embedded in a ball as guides, or observation or identification purposes, provided the designs are flush with the outer surface of the ball. There shall be no interior voids and the plugs or designs must be of a material similar to, although not exactly the same as, the original material out of which the ball was made; and the plugs or designs shall otherwise comply with all bowling ball specifications. No foreign material may be placed on the outer surface of the ball.

Surface Hardness

The surface hardness of a ball shall be not less than 72 Durometer "D." The use of chemicals, solvents, or other methods to change the surface hardness of the ball is prohibited.

INDEX